IN THE SERVICE OF MY COUNTRY

IN THE SERVICE OF MY COUNTRY

I NEVER REGRETTED A DAY

In the Words of Ralph Dykstra

Edited by Larry V. Dykstra

Inspired Forever Books

Dallas, Texas

In the Service of My Country
I Never Regretted a Day

Inspired Forever Books

Dallas, Texas

(888) 403-2727

https://inspiredforeverbooks.com

Words with Lasting Impact

Printed in the United States of America

Library of Congress Control Number: 2016947490

ISBN-13: 978-1-948903-70-7

Cover Design Story

An elderly, Italian man at an American Red Cross building on the Isle of Capri in April 1944 drew this sketch of Tech/Sgt. Ralph Dykstra. About half way through the sitting, a group of B-25 bombers flew overhead at a very low level. "I'm not staying here," the artist said as he ran out the building. He returned a few minutes later to complete the drawing, which was later sent to Alice Ahrens back in the United States.

TABLE OF CONTENTS

Foreword..VII

Introduction: Lessons in Geography...............................1

Chapter One: Something That Had to Be Done.............7

Chapter Two: Trains and Training...............................13

Chapter Three: No Mercy..19

Chapter Four: A Close-Knit Group.............................23

Chapter Five: Uncharted Waters................................31

Chapter Six: Facing Reality..39

Chapter Seven: He Never Knew What Hit Him..........45

Chapter Eight: Playing a Numbers Game......................51

Chapter Nine: Death and Destruction All Around.......57

Chapter Ten: Taking Flak......................................61

Chapter Eleven: A Long Wait..............................67

Chapter Twelve: Soldiers Aren't Supposed to Cry......73

Chapter Thirteen: Close Calls.............................77

Chapter Fourteen: War Is a Sad Experience.................83

Chapter Fifteen: A Sight I Will Never Forget...............91

Chapter Sixteen: Adjusting to Stateside.........................97

Chapter Seventeen: A Birthday Gift for Alice............105

Chapter Eighteen: A Bouquet of Lilies.........................111

Chapter Nineteen: Beating the Odds...........................117

Chapter Twenty: I Never Regretted a Day.................125

Afterword: "These Are the Skies"...............................129

FOREWORD

"Memories, pressed between the pages of my mind..." lyrics from a song popularized by Elvis Presley remind us we are shaped by the experiences of life, and these experiences provide the currency by which memories are acquired. They linger in those pages of our minds, the good ones and the not so good ones, and we don't always know or control when they show up to say hello.

The "Memories" songwriters describe the good ones this way:

"Quiet thoughts come floating down and settle softly to the ground

Like golden autumn leaves around my feet,

I touched them and they burst apart with sweet memories."

But there are other memories, not of quiet thoughts floating down, but of fuse bombs raining down upon allied bombers from German World War II fighter planes flying above them, or of enemy flak, where the imagery of gentle carriers of sweet memories softly falling and bursting upon the serendipitous sojourner is reversed with images of artillery shells racing not so gently upward from the ground and exploding with deadly effect.

These are the memories of a soldier, a soldier commissioned in the noble mission of defending liberty and freedom, and wedded to a flying machine designed for the sole purpose of delivering death and destruction, and opposed by other flying machines and artillery designed to do the same thing.

The images we have of these soldiers are buttressed by the Hollywood screenwriters. This crafted image is not unlike how sons view their fathers – older, wiser, bigger, stronger, capable of all feats the undeveloped mind can create. This caricature was fully expressed in my person, where dads are special, whether they put you on a John Deere tractor at age 13 making you king of the world, or share the memories of life and death stories of a world war fought in the skies over Europe. Absent from this caricature was any notion of a teenage patriot who chose to leave his home and his family to serve his country.

Epiphanies catch us by surprise and they jolt us as they usher in a new thought, idea or perspective. Such was my experience in midlife when one came to me. For no particular reason, in no particular special place on no particularly special day, I found myself thinking of my youngest son, Jonathan, who at the time was twenty years old. And for a moment, I saw him in my mind's eye not as my young son but as my father, the teller of all those fascinating stories. In that moment, the older, wiser, stronger image of my father as a soldier was transformed to that of a person whose boyhood had not quite left him and who would soon be called upon to react to circumstances and events that would demand much more from him than his tender years were prepared to deliver.

The stories of that young soldier open before us in the pages that follow, and they convey experiences from the mundane to the extraordinary. They are written from the perspective of someone having lived a long and full life, but to be fully understood, must be read as experienced by a young man being in the constant stress of war, believing in his cause and joined in that effort by others of like mind and passion. And yes, they are the stories of my dad, whom I love.

Curtis L. Dykstra

March 2016

INTRODUCTION

Lessons in Geography

Geography struck me as an innocent enough subject. The world maps hanging in my fourth-grade classroom introduced me to lines and shapes that defined the countries we studied, places far from the farmlands where I was born and raised. I never expected I would ever see them. The same could probably be said for most children growing up in America in the 1930s.

For my nine classmates and me, our travel horizons extended no farther than small neighboring towns or, at most, to Chicago, seventy miles to the north. Wichert, Illinois, was isolated, innocent, safe, and friendly, so we felt little need or desire to venture far from it. We lived as neighbors in a community tightly woven together by a common Dutch ancestry, Christian faith, and our work as farmers.

A few years later, a global conflict brought more serious lessons in geography into our homes. The border lines we studied that delineated one country from its neighbor had been ignored and rearranged by the human drive for power. A great war started in faraway Europe that challenged not only our understanding of geography but also what was required of us as Americans.

I traveled to Europe ten years after those fourth-grade geography lessons, not as a tourist but as an American soldier. When I arrived there, the country names were familiar but their boundaries had been redrawn by the force of a soulless war machine. I never got to know those countries, their people, or their cultures, only the terrain from my view from the skies high overhead.

I am a veteran of the Second World War. I enlisted in the Army Air Corps at the age of nineteen because I felt it was something I needed to do in support of the cause of freedom. I observed the destruction of buildings from altitudes that reached over 20,000 feet. I witnessed the awful deaths of dear friends from only a few feet away. I saw acts of heroism, cowardice, courage, fear, and compassion. I lived in the crosshairs of death for six intense months. I saw more, felt more, feared more in that short period of time than any other time in my ninety-three years on this Earth. I suffered but survived, and I never regretted a day.

It was decades before I shared much about my war experiences with others. Early on, I told a few stories I knew family and friends would listen to without glancing away or trying to change the subject. But the real stories, the ones that went to the heart of the matter and that mattered most, remained locked inside, out of sight but never out of my mind. That is how I imagine most veterans handle their memories of war — with silence.

It was the geography lesson I was sharing with my thirteen-year-old granddaughter that cracked open the first pages of the unspoken chapters inside me. On Christmas Day of 1988, I was given a world atlas as a gift. Later that day, I was sitting on the couch with Emily, pointing out where I had been on this holiday 45 years earlier when my daughter-in-law, Sandy, said, "You should write something about your combat missions."

"Forget it," I replied. End of story, I thought.

But Sandy called me a couple days later and said, "I think your son Larry would really appreciate it if you would write about your war experiences." That is what started the whole ball rolling.

While my wife, Alice, was at work during the day, I sat in our living room and thought about the people I met and the experiences we shared together during the war. Helped by a copy of my official flight record, I started writing down my memories.

That practical gift of a world atlas offered an invitation that opened my heart to sharing what I saw, felt, feared, and longed for during my time in the service of my country. By accepting that invitation, I received an even greater gift of understanding who I am, what I believe, and how greatly I have been blessed.

The original version of this memoir was my Christmas gift to my three children and their families one year later. The first page inside each copy read:

"It has been some fifty years since Germany, under the leadership of Adolf Hitler, invaded Poland and World War II began. The military personnel of the United States Armed Forces who fought in that war grow fewer in number as time goes by so I decided to write a short autobiography dealing mainly with my time spent in the United States Air Force. My hope is that generations to come may understand that the cause of freedom we enjoy today was bought by the blood and lives of many Americans."

What follows is a revised version of that work. The original stories have been expanded and new ones added. While much of the text has changed, my deepest hope remains the same: that generations to come may understand that the freedom we enjoy today was bought by the blood and lives of many Americans.

My participation in that war molded me into who I am today — a husband, a father, a grandfather, an American, and a child of God. I celebrate the fact that I was born into this world at a time when I could answer the call to make it a safer one.

I am Ralph Dykstra — a proud veteran of World War II. Here is my story.

Lessons in Geography

Central Europe

SCALE IN MILES

CHAPTER ONE

Something That Had to Be Done

As I reflect back on my life, it is interesting to note how the timing of one's birth and the events happening in the world at that time can change the course of one's life so drastically.

I was born the eighth of nine children on March 7, 1923 to Henry and Kate Hoekstra Dykstra. I was raised in the small farming community of Wichert, located about seventy miles south of Chicago, made up of Dutch immigrants. My parents were rather poor people, but at that time most people in the area were poor. The stock market crash in 1929 was followed by the Great Depression in the early 1930s. I don't know how much money my parents held in the bank in the nearby town of St. Anne, but one day, the bank closed all its accounts. Years later, the bank paid back a very small percentage of return on those accounts.

My dad (or "Pa" as we called him) was a large chicken farmer, and we lived well in spite of the tough times. The high levels of unemployment during the Great Depression forced many men to ride the rails in search of jobs. Our home was located a short distance from railroad tracks, and hobos would use secret signs, like rocks placed on fence posts, to mark farmhouses known to be friendly to them. While others were afraid to feed the hobos, I saw Mom serve many meals to those who stopped by our house. She was a generous and caring person who never got too excited about anything.

Pa and Mom urged upon me the importance of church attendance. Biblical instruction was something each one of their children received. My desire was to become a baseball player. I did not attend high school. My older brothers Neil and Rich were married, and brother Bob worked at the tile yard in St. Anne. At the age of fourteen, I was the oldest son at home, and Pa needed help with his chicken farm, so that's what I did. He owned a thousand laying hens, and everything on the farm was done manually. We used a grinder to make our own feed, changed the straw in the laying nests, and picked the eggs by hand each day. It wasn't so much a conscious decision on my part to *not* go to high school.

It was simply the fact that there was work to be done at home.

My teenage years were spent dating a few girls and attending movies. I enjoyed strolling through the large wooded area across the road from our house with my 22 caliber rifle. I became a very accurate shot, using tin cans and bottles for target practice.

In 1936, the storm clouds of war began to form over the continent of Europe. Adolf Hitler rose to power in Germany and, within a few short years, built a military power greater than anything the world had seen. Hitler had served in the German army during World War I and never reconciled to the fact that Germany surrendered, giving up a lot of territory that originally belonged to the country. His goal was to conquer the world. And, for a few years, it seemed he would accomplish that objective. Historians have written that not since Napoleon Bonaparte has one person so affected world history as did Adolf Hitler.

I will never understand how an Austrian and self-proclaimed artist could rise to such power and captivate the German people to a point where they almost considered him a god. During the late 1930s and early 1940s, the powerful German war machine conquered country after country in Europe with their superior military might. Sometime near 1940, under the leadership of Benito Mussolini, Italy joined forces with Germany to create what became known as the Axis powers.

In July 1940, Hitler unleashed Germany's air power to bomb several cities in England. Records show that from July through October, England lost about 900 aircraft, mainly their superb Spitfire and Hurricane fighters. I don't think enough can be written about the courage displayed by the British fighter pilots during that time. Years later, when addressing the House of Commons, England's Prime Minister Winston Churchill paid a great tribute to the pilots of the British Royal Air Force when he said, "Never in the field of human conflict was so much owed by so many to so few."

In March of 1941, I registered for the military draft. All males were required to register on or before their eighteenth birthday. Near the end of that year, I wanted to enlist into a specific branch of the military, preferably the United States Marine Corps. But I had developed abdominal problems that would flair up every month or two, causing me to get sick. I needed my dad's signature to enlist but Pa said, "I'm not signing for you until you get your stomach problems taken care of." At that time, the war seemed a long way away from the United States.

I went to Doc Benjamin, the family doctor and surgeon in St. Anne, who told me I should have my appendix removed. I was recuperating at St. Mary's Hospital in Kankakee when the Japanese attacked Pearl Harbor on December 7, 1941.

The Japanese struck a severe blow to the United States when they destroyed a large portion of our Navy at Pearl Harbor. Our country and its military strength had virtually been brought to its knees by this sneak attack. President Roosevelt, when addressing the nation, stated that December 7, 1941 would be "a date which will live in infamy." Hitler was overjoyed with the news of the attack on Pearl Harbor because we had been sending military aid to England. Four days later, Germany and Italy declared war on the United States.

I stayed home the rest of 1942 until work was done on the farm. In November, I went to the recruiting office in Kankakee and enlisted in the United States Army Air Corps where Pa signed for me. When Pa and I arrived back home, we were greeted by my Aunt Jo and Uncle James Van Schaarderburg, who were visiting from Chicago. Inside the house, Mom was standing by the stove, cooking dinner. She asked how soon I would be leaving, and I replied, "In two days." She began to cry.

I'm sure it had to be tough on all parents to see their sons go off to war, especially as the newspapers described how the German war machine was overrunning Europe. I enlisted with the Army Air Corps (the forerunner to the United States Air Force, which was created in 1947) because I knew I was going to be drafted eventually and would not have been able to pick the branch of service I wanted at that time. I enlisted because I felt it was something that had to be done.

I didn't know what I was getting into.

CHAPTER TWO

Trains and Training

A day or two before I left for basic training, I attended a basketball game at St. Anne High School. In order to save electricity, the games were played during the day. I saw Alice Ahrens there and asked if I could take her home after the game. We had dated several times before, but it was nothing serious. We enjoyed each other's company and agreed to correspond just to keep in touch.

My dad drove me to the Kankakee train station on the morning of November 20, 1942. We were less than a mile down the road when he said, "Son, I'm gonna tell you something. There are a lot of loose women running around those Army camps, so you behave yourself!"

Along with seven other men from the area, I boarded a train bound for the induction center in Chicago where I had my physical. I was sworn into the United States Army Air Corps later that day and stayed overnight in a nearby hotel. In the evening, Dale Irps from St. Anne and I went to see the movie *Holiday Inn* starring Bing Crosby. The song "White Christmas" became popular from that movie.

The next morning, we left for Camp Grant in Rockford, Illinois, where we stayed for about a week getting shots, having our blood type taken, being issued uniforms, and receiving Army-approved haircuts. I was shocked to see what I looked like after all my nice, wavy hair had been cut off. We looked like a bunch of skin heads. A former member of the National Guard showed me how to make my bed to suit Army regulations. He also suggested I keep my billfold under my pillow at night for safekeeping. I was given a set of dog tags to wear around my neck at all times, containing personal information: serial number (16147255), blood type, and home address.

Late one evening, we boarded a troop train without knowing our destination. By the next morning, we realized we were headed to a warmer climate because the snow began to disappear. We had left Camp Grant on Thanksgiving Day dressed in heavy winter uniforms due to the cold weather, but when we arrived at Keesler Field in Biloxi, Mississippi, the temperature was in the low eighties. We walked two miles in a heavy downpour, carrying barracks bags, which contained our clothing.

I began my six weeks of basic training in Biloxi, living with five other soldiers in a tent. I learned very quickly what strict Army discipline was all about: how to take orders, not talk back, march in time, make a bed to Army regulations, wash my own clothes, shine my own shoes, and address everyone who was my superior as "sir." Even though I didn't have a beard, I also learned how to shave. The Army did not allow soldiers to have what they called "peach fuzz."

During this six-week period, we were restricted to the base with no passes to town. Lights were out every night at nine o'clock, and we were up at five in the morning for roll call. We marched everywhere we went. Homesickness was something I never experienced, but sometimes, especially at night, I could hear men crying.

After we completed basic training, we were moved into a wooden barracks, thankful to get out of "tent city" where we slept on old canvas cots. Our barracks was a two-story building about sixty feet long and thirty feet wide with two rows of bunks near the outside walls and an aisle up the middle. Each bed had a spring base and a mattress. We were given foot lockers for our personal belongings, which made it much easier to keep our clothes neat and clean. We were living in style!

At Biloxi, I volunteered to become an aerial gunner and began my training in airplane mechanics. I studied hard and enjoyed learning about altimeters, bank and turn indicators, flaps, ailerons, rudders, and anything else pertaining to aircraft they could cram into this short course. After our final test, I received my diploma on April 11, 1943. A few days later, about sixty men were selected to attend advanced mechanical training at Willow Run, a converted Ford Motor Company plant in Ypsilanti, Michigan, where B-24 bombers were manufactured. I was one of those select few.

On the trip to Ypsilanti, we again had no idea what route we were taking. I don't know why there was so much secrecy everywhere we went. One of the guys on this trip was a short Greek fellow we called "Little Pete," who seemed to spend most of his Army pay on beer or some other alcoholic beverage. During the night, our train stopped in a railway yard to replenish the water and coal supplies. We had no idea where we were until Little Pete looked out the window and said, "We're in Cincinnati." When we asked how he knew, he said he had been through these same rail yards many times in civilian life. In those days, one would have referred to Little Pete as a hobo, but today some might call him a transient worker because he spent his summers in the north and winters in the south. Little Pete was just one of the many different types of individuals I met in the Army, people I never would have met otherwise.

We arrived in Ypsilanti on the twentieth of April. Here, we were schooled in the entire construction and workings of a B-24. We learned about engine overhauls and hydraulic systems, which operated the landing gears, brakes, flaps, and some of the gun turrets. I enjoyed watching the aircraft being assembled here. It was interesting to see women, many weighing less than a hundred pounds, working in the outer edge of the wing section, using a rivet gun to fasten the wing surface to the bulkhead. This area was too small for the average man to comfortably work in, so they had women do the job.

During my stay at Ypsilanti, I was given a three-day pass good for up to 150 miles from the base. As we headed out, I'm sure the military police on the train were aware of the fact that many of us were beyond the distance our pass allowed, but they did not bother us. I went home to visit my parents, of course, but mainly to see Alice, the gal I was falling in love with through our letters.

CHAPTER THREE

No Mercy

After graduating from mechanics school at Willow Run on May 20, 1943, I was transferred to Laredo Army Air Field in Texas for aerial gunnery training. I had been promoted to the rank of corporal, which meant my pay was sixty-six dollars a month.

At Laredo, I experienced some of my toughest military training, with six to eight hours of class and a rigorous physical fitness program each day. We marched double time wherever we went. During inspections each Saturday, we stood at attention beside our bunks. A demerit could be given for a number of reasons, such as improper dress, shoes not shined, bed not made properly, face not cleanly shaven, or hair too long. Receiving a demerit usually meant being assigned to guard duty during off hours. The main purpose for the rigid training and high expectations here was to make us stronger soldiers, both physically and mentally. Some of the guys washed out of the program; they couldn't handle it.

In gunnery school, I learned how a machine gun operated and about the theory of ballistics. I also experienced my first airplane flight in an AT-6, a two-seated airplane with the gunner's seat facing the rear. Pilots would take us up, and we would shoot one hundred rounds of ammunition at a long wind sock being towed by another airplane. The tips of the bullets painted different colors recorded how well we hit the target.

The pilot whose name I drew for my first flight took no mercy on me. He asked if I had ever flown in an airplane before. "No," I replied.

"There's nothing to it," he said. We took off, and when we neared the plane towing the target, he signaled me to begin shooting. I unbuckled my safety belt and hooked my gunner's belt through my parachute harness so I could not fall out. I stood up, swung the machine gun around to the side of the plane, locked it in position, and fired all the ammunition at the target.

The last round was barely out of the gun barrel when the pilot turned the aircraft upside down and plunged us straight down toward the Rio Grande River, throwing me either half in or half out of my seat. Less than 500 feet above the river, he pulled out of the dive, slamming me down in the seat. After we landed, I stepped out of the plane and tossed my cookies. I was ready to tell them to take their program and shove it.

I walked back to the operations building and heard the announcement, "Gunner 404 (my number). You're up in airplane number ..." I walked out to that plane and the pilot said, "You look green." I explained what had happened, and he said he would take it easy on me, which he did. Airsickness was never again a problem for me.

One of the members of our class who could not cope with flying was a fellow named Ed. He was about thirty-eight years old when he was drafted into the service. Ed had never married and many of us referred to him as "Pops." Upon landing from his first flight, Ed walked into the flight operations office and said, "You can court martial me, put me in the stockade, or you can shoot me, but you will never get me back into one of those planes again." The Army discontinued his training and I assume sent him to another air base to work as a mechanic.

I graduated from gunnery school and was proud of that accomplishment. I received my diploma and gunner's wings at an impressive graduation ceremony. I was promoted to the rank of sergeant. I was now making the great sum of seventy-eight dollars a month.

Shortly after graduation, I left for Salt Lake City, Utah. For some reason, our train stopped in the salt flats of Utah. As far as my eye could see, there was absolutely nothing. No vegetation at all, only hard earth baked white by the heat. Having grown up surrounded by fertile Illinois farmland, I had never seen anything so desolate in my life.

My stay at Salt Lake City was brief, only long enough to be processed, issued new clothing, and reassigned. I left a few days later for Gowen Air Force Base near Boise, Idaho, where I would meet the members of my bomber crew.

CHAPTER FOUR

A Close-Knit Group

Our goal in Boise was to become better acquainted with the operation of the B-24 and the duties of each crew member. The officers were Lt. George W. Nix, Pilot; Lt. Dudley Fields, Co-Pilot; Lt. Paul Busse, Bombardier; and Lt Gerald Bush, Navigator. The enlistees included Staff Sgt. Archie Hatch, Nose Gunner; Staff Sgt. Henry A. Barrett, Top Turret Gunner; Staff Sgt. Shannon P. McHenry, Flight Engineer; Staff Sgt. Ralph Burns, Ball Turret Gunner; Corporal Norman Mongeon, Radio Operator and Left Waist Gunner; and Staff Sgt. Ralph Dykstra (me), Tail Turret Gunner. We were ten young men from different parts of the country, getting ready to go to war. Some of us were not even old enough to vote.

23

As part of our training, we were sent to auxiliary landing strips to practice take-offs and landings. Several crashes occurred during this time due to lack of experience flying four-engine aircraft, poor maintenance, or both. Most of the pilots and co-pilots at this base had never flown anything larger than a single or twin engine airplane. Here, I realized what capable men we had in our pilot Lt. Nix and co-pilot Lt. Fields.

We left Gowen Air Force Base in late September for Muroc Army Air Field in California. (Today, it is known as Edwards Air Force Base, where the space shuttles landed.) On the train from Idaho to California, our evening meal was Chicken à la King. Something must have been wrong with the food because many of the guys came down with a severe case of diarrhea, better known in the Army as the "GI Sh---." Imagine the mess with about eighty men per coach and only two "johns." Many relieved themselves between the rail cars. I don't believe in the history of this country, there was ever another railroad right-of-way strewn with so many pairs of undershorts. I can look back at this experience today and chuckle, but at that time it was far from hilarious.

We arrived at Muroc on October 1, 1943 as the beginning of the 456th Heavy Bombardment Group under the command of Colonel Steed, who called us his "Flying Colts." Each squadron had 18 airplanes and 22 crews. There were four squadrons in our group numbered 744 through 747. We were Crew #2 of the 744th squadron.

Muroc was a very small town with a post office, grocery store, and possibly twenty homes. The air field was built on a dry lake with no vegetation, only mirages that appeared like lakes of water. Our lodging consisted of a small plywood shack that accommodated six men. The officers had similar quarters separate from the enlisted men (referred to as non-commissioned soldiers). But Lt. Bush, our navigator, spent a lot of his free time in our shack. He was a free-spirited guy who seemed to enjoy our company. The Army frowned on this type of behavior, but Bush didn't care too much for rules and regulations.

Our training focused on learning how to operate as a crew. Lt. Nix and Lt. Fields learned how to fly in close formation with other bombers. We took many flights to targets in the middle of nowhere. Our bombs were loaded with sand and just enough explosive to deter-mine how well our bombardier hit the target.

On some training flights, our gun turrets were equipped with cameras. Pilots of Navy Corsairs would make mock attacks on us and we would return fire with our gun cameras. After these flights, we would watch the film to see how accurate the gunners had been. I was a pretty good shot, but it was interesting to see how my accuracy improved over time, which was a good thing because I was beginning to realize that our survival in combat could depend on the accuracy of the gunners.

Our navigator Lt. Bush also received his share of training. On some days, we would be given three or four cities to fly over before returning to our base. We also made a few night flights. I recall flying over huge shipyards in the San Francisco harbor, which must have been a restricted area because their search lights were so bright and powerful, we could read a newspaper in the cockpit at 10,000 feet. We got out of that area in a hurry.

During long training flights, I spent a great deal of time on the flight deck discussing technical aspects of the aircraft with the pilots. When our co-pilot Lt. Fields would leave his seat, Lt. Nix would let me take the controls. It was easy to fly the plane once it was airborne, but I found it difficult to keep it level when attempting sharp turns using the rudders. Flying a four-engine bomber was a great experience. I believe I could have flown the aircraft in an emergency, but I doubt I would have been able to land it.

Because of the amount of schooling I had received and the time I spent with our pilot and co-pilot, I wondered if I might be more qualified than Sgt. McHenry for the role of flight engineer. But he was much older than me, and the truth was, I wanted to fly tail turret. But I learned a lot about the flight engineer's job. One of his most important tasks was adjusting the pitch of the propellers by listening to the sound of the engines. Once we reached the proper altitude, we would adjust the pitch of the props so the engines would run smoothly. The flight engineer also understood details about the hydraulic system and how it controlled functions of the aircraft. The pilot and co-pilot had limited knowledge of these things.

Through our combat training, our bomber crew became an efficient fighting force and a close-knit group in a short period of time. After training together for four months, we were almost like brothers. However, Sgt. McHenry never seemed to fit in. He griped about everything. We all tolerated him, but he never showed the enthusiasm the rest of us shared.

Our training was likely cut short due to the need for bomb groups to hit targets in southeastern Europe. Churchill pushed for bomber bases there to attack what he called "the soft underbelly of Europe" because the 8th Air Force based in England couldn't reach targets like the Ploesti Oil Fields in Romania. The upper echelon questioned our commanding officer on whether we were ready for combat. He responded positively, but later realized that we could have used more training. Personally, I didn't think were prepared to go to war, but maybe we never really could be.

Regardless, we were headed to combat with the goal of completing thirty-five missions before we could return home. Near the end of November 1943, four crews in our squadron were flown to Hamilton Field near San Francisco to pick up our new airplanes. We were excited about being assigned the latest model B-24H as our aircraft.

The B-24 Liberator was designed to carry a heavier bomb load with a longer range than the B-17 Flying Fortress. The B-17 was the first four-engine bomber developed by the United States and was used heavily during the early stages of the war. When military leaders realized the advantages of the B-24, nicknamed the "Flying

Boxcar" based on the look of its fuselage, it became the workhorse of the U.S. Air Force. Records indicate that over 19,000 B-24s were built for combat compared to 12,000 B-17s, but the B-17 received more recognition because it was based primarily in Great Britain where many American press members were stationed early in the war.

In early December, I received a letter from either Pa or my sister Millie sharing the bad news that Mom was sick. I didn't know how serious it was at the time. I was only twenty years old and I didn't know much about cancer, so I wasn't too concerned at first. Pa contacted the Red Cross in an attempt to get me home on emergency leave to see her, but the Army said there would be no furloughs or leaves given to any of us since we were scheduled to head overseas in about two weeks. This upset a lot of the men because we were given no opportunity to say good-bye to loved ones.

McHenry was particularly distressed by this decision to halt furloughs. He complained to anyone who would listen. He told our superior officers, "You might as well fly a sack of potatoes overseas because that's how much help I plan to be there."

From Hamilton Field, we made a number of stops on our flight across the United States from Palm Springs, California, to West Palm Beach, Florida. A co-pilot on one of the crews knew our route from Midland, Texas, to Memphis, Tennessee, would take us over his home town of about four thousand in Arkansas. He phoned his wife the night before we left Midland telling her we would be passing over the next day. When we flew over at very low level and in tight formation, it looked like the whole town had congregated in the school yard where she taught, waving American flags and banners. It was a thrilling sight, almost like a personal send-off.

From Memphis, we flew to West Palm Beach where we waited for the orders that would begin our journey overseas. On the night of December 21, 1943, I stood in a long line of soldiers with a pocket full of quarters, waiting to use a pay phone to call home. Since my parents did not have a telephone, I called my brother Neil so he could tell them I would be leaving the United States soon. I sent a Western Union telegram to Alice at St. Mary's Hospital, where she was training to be a nurse. It read: LOVE AND BEST WISHES FOR CHRISTMAS AND THE NEW YEAR. RALPH DYKSTRA.

CHAPTER FIVE

Uncharted Waters

Early on the morning of December 22, 1943, we left the continental United States with a sealed packet of orders and a navigational course to fly for two to three hours before opening it. Our landing gear was barely off the ground when Lt. Nix told us to open the packet. I always kidded him about that. "What would you have done if we had engine trouble and had to turn back?" I asked.

"We'd have managed somehow to get out of that," he said.

Some members of the crew hoped our destination would be the Pacific War Zone. Others were hoping for Europe. I really had no preference. Regardless of our assignment, I'm sure each of us felt a gnawing fear inside over what lay ahead.

The following morning, we landed on Trinidad, an island just off the northeastern coast of Venezuela. We spent the next day resting from our long night flight and the excitement that accompanied leaving the United States. We were proud of Lt. Bush who navigated us directly over the airfield where we landed.

On Christmas Eve, we took off for another long flight to Belém, Brazil, with two additional passengers on board: crew chief and head mechanic Sgt. Nielsen and Lt. Jackson, the pilot of a different crew. Lt. Jackson was flying with us because his crew had not been assigned a plane. Each squadron was comprised of twenty-two crews but only eighteen airplanes. On bombing missions, the additional crews would fly a plane belonging to a crew that was not scheduled to fly that day. I felt sorry for the crews who did not have a plane they could call their own.

On Christmas Day, we flew six more hours to Natal, Brazil. This geographical location provided the shortest route across the Atlantic to Africa. We were treated there to a wonderful Christmas dinner, although not as nice as what Mom would have cooked. Some used to say, "Kate Dykstra could make a great meal out of nothing." But for Army chow, our dinner was as good as could be expected. In the afternoon, we relaxed in the warm sunshine on the beach at the edge of the Atlantic Ocean. We talked about how great it would have been to spend the day at home with our families. I thought about my mother who was celebrating her 58th birthday that very day.

We remained in Brazil longer than expected due to a severe tropical storm that developed over the Atlantic between South America and Africa. While we waited, I enjoyed eating my share of fresh pineapple and bananas. One day, our radio operator, Archie Hatch, decided he needed a drink, so he gave a ten-dollar bill to a local kid who was hanging around our base and asked him to buy a bottle of cognac. The boy returned an hour later with a single bottle. An American civilian who was working on the base saw this and asked Archie how much money he had given the boy. When Archie told him, the man spoke to the boy and sent him back to town. A couple hours later, the boy returned and gave Archie a second bottle of cognac and five dollars in change.

We assembled early in the morning of January 5, 1944, for our flight across the Atlantic. The gas tanks were filled to capacity with 2,700 gallons of fuel. We were told the tropical storm over the ocean had dissipated, but we ran into it during our flight. The winds tossed our plane about like a toothpick. Unable to rise above the storm, the pilot and navigator decided to go around it, creating some anxious moments due to the increase in fuel consumption this tactic required.

I recall the crew's sense of relief when our nose gunner announced the sight of land from his forward position. Once again, our navigator, Lt. Bush, had come through with flying colors, taking us directly over the air base where we were to land. I never understood how he did this given the heavy cloud cover and no navigational points to pick up over the water. With today's GPS technology, this would be fairly easy. But in 1944, it seemed like a miracle. When we arrived over Dakar, Africa, we had only fifty gallons of gas left for each engine, which left us with little remaining flying time. Our trip across the Atlantic had taken almost thirteen hours, more than half a day.

Before we left Natal, a native offered to sell a monkey to our crew for twenty-five bucks. Some of the guys decided to buy it, but I wanted no part of this deal. These monkeys were pesky little things that would hop around and sit on your shoulder. The same native overcharged us for a bushel of bananas to feed the darn thing. I had no love for this monkey. The only good thing that came from this deal was that I got to eat more bananas than the monkey on our flight across the ocean.

From Dakar, we flew for almost eight hours to Marrakesh, Morocco, where we stopped for rest and refueling. When we landed in the heat of the day, we were issued three wool blankets. I didn't understand why they gave us such heavy blankets, but that night, as the cold settled in, I found out why. Despite wearing my heavy flight suit under all three blankets, I still found it too cold to sleep. I didn't realize it could get so cold in the desert.

On the morning of January 9, 1944, we gathered for takeoff to Tunis (the capital of Tunisia) in North Africa. Part of our normal procedure was to turn the engines over by what was called "pulling the props." But on that morning, the engines were so cold, the propellers wouldn't budge. We had to drain the oil out of the tanks and use heaters to warm it up in order to start the engines.

The flight to Tunis was uneventful, up until the point when we were unable to find the airfield where we were supposed to land. We flew over the harbor area where American and British war ships were anchored. Perhaps mistaking us for the enemy, they sent up warning shots of anti-aircraft fire. Needless to say, we made a fast exit from the area and eventually found the airfield that would be our temporary base.

It took weeks before the entire 456th Heavy Bombardment Group was assembled at Tunis. Three other planes developed mechanical problems and were delayed for repairs. One crew had to wait four weeks until a new engine could be sent and changed out. We found out later, after the entire group formed in North Africa, that a couple crews from another squadron apparently ran out of fuel and were forced to ditch in the Atlantic. To my knowledge, they were never found or rescued.

During our wait in North Africa, we made short training flights and kept in good physical condition. One day, the pet monkey got into ball turret gunner Burns' equipment while we were away. A couple days later, the monkey disappeared. We all suspected Sgt. Burns, but he never admitted he had any part in it. Even though I hated that dumb monkey, at least it wasn't me who got rid of him.

In time, more equipment began to arrive: gasoline, ammunition, bombs, and tents. We would soon be headed into combat.

Two weeks after we arrived at Tunis, I was told to report to the office of our flight operations officer Captain Ladd. He said, "I'm making you flight engineer on your bomb crew."

"I don't want to be the flight engineer," I said. I felt I was a pretty good tail gunner, and I knew the rear of the plane would be one of our most vulnerable positions during combat, so I thought I could best help the crew if I remained in that role.

"I don't give a damn what you want," Captain Ladd answered. "You're the flight engineer!" He then gave me a very strong lecture, saying it was up to me to pull our crew together or we would not last long in combat. I was promoted to the rank of Tech/Sgt. and given another stripe, making me a "five striper."

Later, our crew learned that Lt. Nix removed Sgt. McHenry from his position for "failure to obey orders." Apparently, he refused to fly. He gave no reason, but I believe he turned chicken. We all feared what was ahead, but there is a vast difference between being afraid and being a coward. Sgt. McHenry was demoted to the rank of private and immediately removed from our quarters. This episode upset the entire crew, but McHenry never did fit in, so maybe it was for the best. I felt sorry for him, but the decision not to fly was his, and he would have to live with it.

CHAPTER SIX

Facing Reality

In early 1944, allied troops pushed the German and Italian armies to a line about fifty miles north of Foggia, Italy. Our entire bomb group was moved to an airstrip a few miles south of the city that had been used by the Germans. When we arrived at our airfield, we couldn't believe there was only one gravel runway. U.S. troops hooked together large steel pads about a half inch thick and six feet by two feet in size at the end of the airstrip. This surface provided our planes a secure spot for an initial touch down when landing. The loud racket we made on our crew's first landing on these steel pads almost scared me to death.

During our first few nights in Italy, we slept under the stars in our flight suits. When all was quiet, we could hear heavy artillery being fired across the front line. We were each issued a Thompson sub-machine gun to use in case of a German counter attack. We were getting closer to the war.

Tents eventually arrived, but living conditions were still crude here. Because the nights were cold, we built a heating system inside our tent made from a fifty-gallon drum cut in half with rocks piled in the center. A pipe sticking up through the top of the tent served as a chimney. Outside the tent sat a tank of gasoline with a piece of metal tubing entering the drum and rock piles. We would light a piece of paper and turn a valve that allowed the gasoline to drip slowly on the pile of rocks, producing heat for our tent. It wasn't the safest set-up, but it worked, unless someone forgot to shut the valve before trying to light the gas source. On a couple occasions, we heard a loud "Vroom" from a nearby tent. A few guys got singed but no one was seriously injured.

Shortly after we arrived in Italy, every member of our group was sent on an orientation flight to familiarize us with the area. Our ability to identify landmarks from the air would help us find our way back to the base when returning from a mission. We were stationed south of the small village of Cerignola, and on days when the sun was shining, we could see the dome of its Catholic church from miles away.

Three pilots and a flight engineer took off on one of these orientation flights on one cloudy day. They may have interpreted the height of the mountains in yards instead of meters. A meter is only slightly longer than a yard, by a little more than three inches. But this small difference becomes a very large one when multiplied by the thousands. As a result of this mistake, their flying altitude was too low and they crashed into a mountainside, killing them all. Our pilot, Lt. Nix, had trained with all three pilots and was good friends with them. Our group hadn't flown a single mission yet, but we were already suffering major casualties.

On February 17, 1944, we flew our first mission to bomb the German High Command Headquarters north of Rome. We had no fighter escort at this time, and the same would be true for many missions to come. I remember seeing a German ME-110 flying beyond gun range along the left side of our formation. The pilot in that plane would radio our altitude and air speed to the German anti-aircraft batteries to improve the accuracy of their flak attacks. In other words, they provided the artillery units on the ground with our positioning information so they knew where to fire their exploding shells. Our group had been told this would be an easy mission, but we still lost three planes due to flak and enemy fighters.

When we arrived back at the base, I told ball turret gunner Burns we would never make it to thirty-five missions. When he asked why, I pointed out that each squadron had put up nine planes that day and three were shot down. We were supposed to do this thirty-five times, so the odds were against us. I was not making light of our situation, just attempting to face reality.

On our missions to targets that were vital to Germany's war machine, as many as three hundred bombers would take part. We could tell how important the target was to Germany based on how well it was defended — by the number of enemy fighters and the amount of flak we met. On other days, smaller groups of bombers would strike several different targets at almost the same time.

When we weren't scheduled to fly, we were free to do as we pleased. We built a recreation hall where we passed the time with other bomb crews. It was a nice building with walls of stone and a roof made from tents sewed together. For bathing facilities, we used our steel helmets. Eventually, we confiscated some large metal tanks, put them up on tall poles, and covered them with glass. The sun would warm the water so we could take a shower. I guess you would call it American ingenuity. It still puzzles me where we obtained all this material, but there was always someone who had connections and a way of getting the job done.

Each airplane was given a name by its crew. There were all kinds of names. I remember one plane painted with a heavily endowed gal named "Ophelia Bumps." Our plane was "Madame Zig Zig," which meant something rather vulgar in Italian. Sgt. Busse never asked anybody else on our crew about the name; he just came up with it on his own. He also had a blonde gal painted on it by some Italian guy. Some members of the crew took offense.

As time went by, more bomb groups arrived at our base in Italy. Eventually, there were fifteen bomb groups assigned to the 15th Air Force under the command of General Nathan Twining. On two different occasions, one of our B-24s exploded when the landing gears were raised during takeoff. We never knew for sure why those explosions happened, although some suspected sabotage by someone supporting the German cause. We had already gotten a sense of the danger we faced flying our missions, and these incidents added to the tension. Due to the threat of sabotage and unknown enemies, enlisted men were issued a 45 automatic pistol for protection and assigned to guard the planes at night. Members of the Red Cross would come out around 2 o'clock in the morning and bring us coffee and donuts.

March 7, 1944 was my 21st birthday. We were scheduled to go out on our fourth bombing mission, and the guys kidded that I wouldn't live long as a man. A common saying at the time was, "Staff sergeant today, stiff sergeant tomorrow." That may sound cruel or heartless, but it reflected our view of life at that time. We had quickly learned to live each day as it came. That was our reality.

CHAPTER SEVEN

He Never Knew
What Hit Him

Without a replacement for McHenry, I continued to handle both tail gunner and flight engineer responsibilities. This was not the best way to operate, but there were no available replacements qualified to fill in as tail gunner, which was probably the most vulnerable area of the plane during combat. I requested they fill McHenry's position of flight engineer so I could continue flying the tail turret, but Captain Ladd would not hear of it. I covered both positions until a tail turret replacement arrived.

I loved the tail turret. It operated hydraulically and would move laterally about fifty degrees to the right or left. The up and down movement of the guns operated the same way. There were two handles about a half arm's length in front of the operator with thumb triggers to press when firing was required. These handles were used to manipulate both the turret and guns. A lighted ring sight turned on by an electrical switch and would move up or down in conjunction with the movement of the guns. The turret was covered by a piece of one-inch-thick glass about 18 by 24 inches in size. This glass was said to be bulletproof, but I doubt it would have stopped a shell from one of the 50-caliber machine guns used by the German fighters.

Each gun was equipped with hundreds of rounds of ammunition held together with metal links. The links and spent shells would fall away outside the turret when the guns were fired. Our links of ammunition usually consisted of one tracer, two incendiary shells, and two armor-piercing shells. After lengthy firing during a mission, the operators had to be careful which direction they pointed their guns because a hot barrel could "cook off" a shell or two on its own and hit one of our own planes.

We flew in formations comprised of six "flights" with six planes in each flight. These flights were named Able, Baker, Charlie, Dog, Easy, and Fox. The Able flight took the lead with Baker slightly behind and to the right, and Charlie slightly behind and to the left. These three flights were called the "first echelon." The other three flights comprised the "second echelon" with

Dog in the middle, Easy to the right, and Fox on the left. The second echelon flew slightly lower than the first echelon to avoid being affected by the turbulence given off by the propellers of Able, Baker, and Charlie.

I was blessed with very good vision, which came in quite handy when we were on the lookout for enemy fighters. On one occasion, I announced over the intercom that I had spotted six German ME 109s approaching in the distance. In disbelief, top turret gunner Barrett responded, "Wipe the fly shit off your turret glass, Dyke." A couple minutes later, Barret confirmed the sighting, "Oh, wait. There they are."

The most dangerous time on any mission was what was known as the bomb run. As we neared the target, each plane in the formation moved closer together, which concentrated our fire power against the enemy fighters and enabled us to make a more accurate bomb drop. Upon reaching the initial point (IP) of the bomb run, we could not deviate from this course or take any evasive action no matter how much flak or enemy fighters we met. A bomb run lasted only five to ten minutes, but each seemed to last an eternity until we heard those two beautiful words "bombs away." After that, we would immediately descend in order to gain air speed so we could get away from the target area as quickly as possible.

Sometimes we would attack our target in smaller groups at different time intervals. When the German fighters challenging the first group of bombers landed to refuel, another group of our B-24s would arrive and catch them on the ground.

As we flew more missions, each one seemed to get worse. We were sent deeper into enemy territory, which gave German fighters more time to attack us on our way to the targets. We also had to deal with flak near our targets; the Germans were becoming experts at this. When we saw those first bursts of black smoke from the anti-aircraft fire directed our way, our nose gunner Archie Hatch would sing out over the intercom the lyrics from a popular song at the time: "That old black magic's got me in its spell." It sounds crazy now, but those were crazy times.

Our crew sustained its first casualty on April 3, 1944. During a raid over a rail yard in Budapest, our navigator, Lt. Bush, was killed. We were not flying our own plane that day because it had been grounded for engine repairs. We were assigned number three position in the Able flight. Enemy flak was intense and accurate and we were hit very hard. We were also met by many Messerschmitt Bf 109 and Focke-Wulf Fw 190 fighters. After we dropped our bombs, we were forced to shut down our #2 engine due to a serious loss of oil pressure. With one engine out, we had to increase the RPMs on the remaining three to stay with the rest of the formation.

When we crossed the Adriatic Sea coastline into Yugoslavia, Lt. Nix decided to leave the formation because we were running our remaining three engines at higher than recommended RPMs, which risked damaging them and creating more serious problems. We dropped to a very low altitude so we would not be detected by enemy fighters, decreased the power on the remaining engines, and continued on alone. When we arrived at our base a half hour or so later than the other crews, we were given quite a welcome. Many thought we wouldn't make it home.

After landing, we inspected the damage to our borrowed aircraft. We counted 274 holes ranging from the size of a dime to three large enough for a man to crawl through. The lower half of the right rudder was completely blown away, which had made it difficult for the pilot and co-pilot to control the aircraft.

I will not go into detail about Lt. Bush's death. He never knew what hit him.

The loss of Lt. Bush was a severe blow to our morale. With this recent loss, we couldn't believe we were scheduled to fly again the next day. When the crew met at the plane after the briefing session, Lt. Nix said, "Dyke, when we get airborne, find something wrong with this crate." He was in no mood to fly. Ironically, our plane developed a leak in the hydraulic system, and we had to return to base.

The next day, our entire crew was sent to the Isle of Capri off the west coast of Italy for rest and rehabilitation. It seemed Lt. Nix needed this more than anyone else. The death of Bush hit Lt. Nix especially hard because he assumed such great responsibility for the safety of his crew.

CHAPTER EIGHT

Playing a Numbers Game

On the Isle of Capri, we stayed in a hotel near the beach, got up in the morning when the spirit moved us, and went to the dining hall any time we wanted during the day for a very good meal. All personnel sent for R&R were treated the same, so we were not required to salute officers of any rank. This was difficult to get used to at first.

Late one afternoon, we met some sailors from a destroyer crew anchored in the harbor. They invited us onboard their ship that evening, where we ate steak — a meal I had not enjoyed since I left home. We were also treated to homemade ice cream for dessert. Compared to the Army, it appeared that the Navy fed their men very well.

When we returned to our base ten days later, we met Lt. Bush's replacement: Wilson D. Smith from Aurora, Illinois. William J. Harvey took over the tail turret position. As flight engineer, my position during combat would be the right waist gun, which allowed me greater freedom to assist the pilot and co-pilot if needed.

When we began flying missions again, we were delighted to learn that we had fighter escorts. These P-38, P-47, and P-51 fighters were able to fly much faster than our bombers, so they would take off after us and catch up over enemy territory. When enemy fighters challenged our bomb groups, the American fighters would attack back.

Fuel levels were always a great concern for the American fighter pilots because during aerial combat, it was consumed very rapidly. On many occasions, our fighter escorts were forced to break off and head for home base for fear of running out of fuel. Usually, another group of fighters that took off later than the first met us over the target to help against the enemy fighters. But sometimes the timing was off, and they would arrive either too early or too late to be of much help or need.

On one of our longer missions into German territory, our protection was a squadron of P-47s, a highly maneuverable aircraft with a powerful engine. The P-47 was equipped with a large, disposable gasoline tank attached to its belly that the plane drew fuel from, so it had a longer flight range and could escort missions deeper into enemy territory. If the P-47 pilots encountered German fighters before this tank was empty, they could jettison the belly tank and still have plenty of fuel to take on the enemy and get back to base.

On this day, our escorts were black American pilots known as the Tuskegee Airmen. I will never forget the courage displayed by this group of pilots as we neared the target. Even though they were highly outnumbered by some of the best German pilots flying ME-109s and Focke-Wulf 190s trying to disrupt our formation, these men outfought them. No one could expect any greater display of fearlessness and daring than this squadron showed on that day. I am sure their skill, bravery, and determination helped keep our bomber losses down considerably. Lt. Nix stated how he wished he could personally thank these Airmen for how superbly they performed.

It is sad to say that at this time in history, segregation was strictly enforced in all branches of the U.S. military. I wonder if I had been in these guys' shoes whether I would have laid my life on the line to protect the lives of men of an all-white bomber group only to return home after the war to a society segregated by skin color. I don't know if anyone connected with this group of P-47 pilots will ever read this, but I want to say, "Thank you" to those "Red Tail Angels" who fought so valiantly that day over some part of Europe. God bless you wherever you are. I will never forget you.

When enemy fighters attacked, we called out on the intercom the direction of the attack based on a clock system where the nose of our aircraft was referred to as twelve o'clock, the right wing three o'clock, the tail six o'clock, and the left wing nine o'clock. For example, if their point of attack was from above the right rear of our aircraft I would call out, "Fighters four o'clock high." Enemy fighters usually approached from the rear of the formation giving them a longer time to fire at us. However, sometimes they would attack from the front, especially at the lead flight, in an attempt to disrupt our formation as we neared the bomb run target.

After we had dropped our bombs on one raid over Klagenfurt, a damaged B-24 from another bomber group flew in close behind our position. I knew this plane was from another group because the lower half of the rudder was painted a different color. I caught sight of a German ME 109 ready to attack the bomber and began firing at it while the crippled B-24 dropped down a couple hundred feet. Instead of going after that bomber, the fighter came directly at us. I continued firing until the ME 109 began to emit black smoke and turned away. Our ball gunner watched the plane go down and saw it crash. No parachute was seen.

On my twenty-sixth mission, tragedy struck again when Sgt. Burns, our ball turret gunner, was killed. We never received a replacement for him. His position was filled on a rotating basis by personnel from other crews.

By now, our graceful old plane was showing many battle scars. It was originally painted Army green, but as damage was repaired, sections of the sheet metal skin were cut away and pieces of shiny new aluminum were riveted in their place.

On the side of each plane, just below the pilot's window, several small bombs were painted, indicating the number of missions that plane had flown. I had flown more missions than the rest of my crew by substituting for wounded flight engineer Sgt. Beland on Crew #4. It seemed they were often scheduled to fly when we were not, which allowed me to get six to eight missions ahead of my crew. My hope was that I could finish my missions earlier and return home in time to see my mom.

It was around this time that the bomber crews were given a new goal. We had been told in California we needed to be credited with thirty-five missions before we could return to the States, but now the number was fifty. I don't know why they raised the target. Most likely, those in command believed our bombing missions were succeeding at destroying enemy targets and they decided to continue them longer than originally planned. Those of us who had been there the longest could see that replacement crews were not arriving fast enough to offset the heavy losses we were suffering. "All they're doing is playing a numbers game on us," said Lt. Fields.

For me, the sad truth was it would take even longer for me to complete my missions and get home to see my mother.

CHAPTER NINE

Death and Destruction
All Around

Ploesti … just the mention of this target struck fear in the heart of every crewman in the 15th Air Force. Huge oil fields and refineries located in this area of Romania supplied forty percent of all Germany's fuel. Missions to Ploesti and nearby targets such as Campina, Giurgiu, Brasov, and Bucharest were always rough ones.

These targets were all heavily defended by a superb group of German fighter pilots, and we could always count on there being heavy flak. Official records indicate that from August 1943 to August 1944, when the twentieth and last raid made on Ploesti completely destroyed the oil refining operations, 223 American bombers were lost. I don't know how many American fighters were also lost, but I believe more crews perished in the effort to destroy these huge oil fields and refineries than any other target in the air war over Europe.

Aircraft scheduled to hit Ploesti would vary their altitude on the bomb run to decrease the accuracy of the anti-aircraft batteries. For example, one group might fly over at 24,000 feet and the next at 19,000 feet. On both of my missions to Ploesti, the sky was literally black with smoke from anti-aircraft fire.

Although it is not included in my official flight records, I recall our mission to Ploesti on May 5, 1944. It is possible that I was flying with another crew that day and my name was not recorded in the log book completed by the crew captain. Because of this omission, I did not receive credit for this flight. Upon returning from the mission, all of the crews in the group reported large rail yards at Campina, about thirty miles away. Estimates ranged from 300 to 500 loaded tanker cars at this location.

When we arrived at Campina on May 6 to attack this target, smoke still lingered at 20,000 feet from our bombing of nearby Ploesti on the previous day. Almost two weeks later, we hit Ploesti again. These flights were all close to eight hours in length, stretching our fuel supply to the limits because of the huge bomb loads we were carrying.

On May 10, 1944, we were sent on a mission to bomb an aircraft factory at Wiener Neustadt* where the

German ME 109 fighters were manufactured. Our crew was again in the lead flight at the #2 position. After we were airborne for a short time, the lead plane developed engine trouble and returned to base. Our plane moved into the #1 position, which meant we were leading the entire bomb group for the first time. While leading the group was certainly an honor, the plane in the lead position always seemed to sustain the heaviest damage. The German fighter pilots knew that the best way to disrupt the entire formation on the bomb run was to attack the lead plane.

The enemy fighters we encountered on this mission were the most terrifying we had ever experienced. Because many planes in our group were hit, the entire formation constantly changed as each vacated position was filled by another crew. During the bomb run into the target, Captain Clark's plane, which had moved into the position vacated by ours, was hit by flak and caught fire. He pulled away from the formation off to our right as flames poured out the bomb bay.

I can still see Captain Clark as clear as I did that day. He looked like he didn't have a care in the world as he struggled to stabilize the bomber long enough for his crew members to get out. He knew his life was about to end, but he sat there as cool as a cucumber. I saw three chutes come out the escape hatch in the back just before the plane disintegrated in an explosion that left nothing but small pieces of the aircraft and burning gasoline tanks falling through the air. I don't know what blew. Maybe the gas tank heated up enough to explode the bombs in the aircraft. Captain Clark had gotten far enough away from the formation to protect the rest of us. Even so, the concussion was enough to shake our plane.

We continued the bomb run and dropped our payload. When we came off the target, I realized we were the only plane left from our flight of six. I had gotten so caught up in the action that I was unaware of the great losses we had sustained. We took cover with another flight to avoid being a lone target for the German fighters.

I cannot find words to express how terrible this whole ordeal was. It seemed that death and destruction was all around us. Planes were constantly leaving the formation — disabled or on fire. Many never reached the target. There were too many parachutes in the air to count.

*Chapter Note:

It was on this mission to Weiner Neustadt that our unit was awarded a Presidential Citation for the damage we had inflicted to this large aircraft factory.

CHAPTER TEN

Taking Flak

How we escaped the anti-aircraft fire we faced on some of our missions, I'll never know. Over heavily defended targets, the sky would often be black with smoke from exploding flak shells. We joked about the flak being so thick we could walk on it.

Benny S. was a radio operator on one of the other original crews in our bomber group. The flight engineer on that crew was either wounded or sick for an upcoming mission, so I was scheduled to fly with them. When we neared the target, I stood at the right waist gun position searching the sky for enemy fighters while Benny manned the gun on the left side of the plane. When I turned around, I was shocked to see Benny sitting on an empty ammunition box, head buried in his hands as he trembled with fear. Every time a flak shell burst close by, the concussion rocked the plane and his whole body shook.

Benny was useless that day as enemy fighters attacked our formation, but I felt a sense of pity for him. We were all afraid and dreaded each burst of flak, but there sat a man too proud to admit fear. I respected Benny more than our crew's former flight engineer, McHenry, who simply refused to fly in combat. I would have to be either the biggest liar in the world or the greatest fool to say I wasn't afraid, but, as I said before, there is a vast difference between being a coward and being afraid.

Around this time, we were given flak suits to wear, which included vests similar to those police wear today. I am certain this vest saved me from a much more severe injury on our mission over Wiener Neustadt. I was knocked over by the force of an explosion, causing my steel helmet to fall into the ball-turret. Later, after he emerged from his position, I remember ball-gunner Barrett saying that he thought someone in the waist section must have been killed. The cloth covering on my flak suit was torn in several places from shrapnel. I had suffered a wound to my left thigh, which I feared was severe because of the pain and amount of blood on my flight suit.

On this mission, our aircraft received serious damage: three huge holes and several small ones. One large hole was on top of the wing section behind the #2 engine. The German fighters would often fly about 2,000 feet above our formation and drop fuse bombs that would explode after falling a predetermined number of feet or upon striking something. I'm sure this is what caused the gaping hole in our wing section, rupturing a fuel tank.

Another huge hole was located in the top of the fuselage, leaving us without an intercom system since all the main radio components located in the bomb bay section were blown to pieces by the explosion. Fortunately, the oxygen tanks located above the bomb section weren't hit. We had a third large hole in the lower section of the fuselage, which, thankfully, did not cause any severe damage.

When one of the large explosions occurred, there was a red flash throughout the aircraft. The radio operator snapped on his chest chute, and I did the same because we expected the plane to catch fire. We had never practiced bailing out of the plane, but we did have a procedure for abandoning the aircraft, which consisted of a series of bell warnings given by the pilot. If the bell rang once, it signaled us to get ready; two rings meant "bail out." The pilot needed to make a quick decision because the chances of escaping from a bomber spiraling out of control were almost nil.

The nose section and tail turret were probably the most difficult areas to abandon. The guys up front were to exit out the nose wheel after they cranked it out. Those of us in the back had an escape hatch in the floor between the waist windows and the tail turret. The pilot, co-pilot, and top turret gunner would exit out the bomb bay doors. We were instructed to count to ten before pulling our ripcords. I had seen men bail out and open parachutes too soon, only to get caught on a part of the plane or have their chute catch on fire.

When another large explosion occurred, I was standing at the right waist gun. I didn't know what part of the plane was hit, so I thought I better take a look to assess the damage. I stuck my head out the left waist window, and the slip stream ripped my oxygen mask from my face. One cannot stay conscious very long at 24,000 feet without oxygen, so I grabbed a portable tank and sucked on a hose periodically until we reached an altitude low enough for me to breathe without it.

The gasoline tanks on the B-24 were located inside the wing section, with one behind each engine and two emergency tanks in the wingtips. These tanks were made of two heavy layers of rubber with some type of sealant between the layers. A small hole would self-seal, but we had a gaping hole with the metal on the outer wing section torn upward. After the enemy fighters broke off their attack, I walked from my waist gun position to the flight deck and told Lt. Nix we should shut down the #2 engine because gasoline was spilling down the wing section directly behind the engine.

Why no fire started, I'll never know. We feathered the prop upon shutting the engine down, meaning we adjusted the propeller blades so they would knife into the air and not windmill, which would cause severe drag on the aircraft. Fuel could be transferred between tanks by turning a series of valves and starting a small transfer pump in the bomb bay section. After the engine was shut down, I used this transfer system to empty the ruptured tank. I can't say how much time this all took, but I'm sure it wasn't too long. Everything happened so quickly up there that you had to react without thinking.

After completing my tasks as flight engineer, I returned to the flight deck and asked Lt. Nix to examine my injury. I removed my flight suit and a pair of long johns, and we found a piece of shrapnel about a half-inch square lodged in my leg. It had passed through two packs of Lucky Strike cigarettes and a small box of matches in a patch pocket of my flight suit. Lt. Nix removed the shrapnel and bandaged my wound using material from one of several first aid kits on the aircraft. It continued to bleed heavily for a short period of time.

My wound took a long time to heal. I returned to the flight surgeon several times over the next few days to have it redressed. The flight surgeon told me I was eligible for the Purple Heart, a medal awarded for shedding blood for your country. I refused because I had seen too many men removed from planes with severe injuries and knew my crewmates Bush and Burns would both receive the award posthumously. Being awarded the same medal for shedding a few drops of blood from a wound leaving a scar that I can hardly find today didn't seem right to me.

Also, if I had accepted the Purple Heart, the War Department would have sent an announcement to my hometown newspaper saying, "Sgt. Ralph Dykstra has been wounded in action." It would have taken me three weeks after that news was printed to get letters to my family and Alice telling them I was okay. My dad had enough "hay on the fork" caring for the farm and my mom, and she didn't need more worries given her condition. They didn't need to read in the newspaper that I was wounded without knowing how serious it was.

Our group did not fly again for eight days following the Wiener Neustadt aircraft factory raid. We had paid dearly in the loss of men and planes.

CHAPTER ELEVEN

A Long Wait

Before each mission, most of the crew attended a briefing session that included maps displaying the target area. Those attending were told what to expect in terms of enemy fighters and anti-aircraft. The nose gunner/armament specialist, Archie Hatch, and I never attended these briefing meetings. Instead, we would be brought out to the aircraft, where Archie would inspect the bomb load, guns, and turrets to make certain everything was in operating condition and that we had enough ammunition. My duties included reviewing a checklist with head mechanic Nielsen to make certain our plane was performing in the best possible operating condition.

On the morning of each mission, we were up before daylight. We would go to the mess hall for a breakfast of French toast with "syrup." (It was sugar water.) I usually found eating nearly impossible due to anxious thoughts about what the day held in store for us. I'd choke down what I could and fly for the next five to eight hours. We were given what was called a K-ration (which usually consisted of a small can of condensed meat, a couple crackers, a fruit or chocolate bar, and three cigarettes) to take on the mission, but eating anything at 20,000 feet while wearing an oxygen mask was near impossible. Most of us ate only the fruit or chocolate bar and would give what was left to the Italian children when we returned to our base. Physically drained after each tough mission, we often returned to our tent following a debriefing session and fell asleep, sometimes missing evening chow. It is easy to see how one could lose considerable weight during this time. I certainly did.

Letters from home were very important to the morale of most of us in the military. We were given an APO (Army Post Office) number of 520 New York, New York, as an address where family, friends, and loved ones could send letters. Mail only arrived once a week, so when we heard "mail call" announced, we would rush to the designated area. Because I came from a large family with very concerned parents and a sweetheart back home. I received many letters. They often arrived in bunches with various postmark dates on them. Some soldiers never received any mail at all.

Before my next mission, I needed to replace the oxygen mask that had been ripped off my face during our mission over Weiner Neustadt. But when I went to the supply depot to get a new one, the sergeant in charge told me I had to sign a statement of charges, which meant the cost would come out of my paycheck. "I lost it on a mission over Wiener Neustadt," I said.

"I can't help it," he said. "You have to sign a statement of charges."

"Well, I'm not signing a statement of charges."

I told Lt. Nix about this and he said, "I'll go with you, Dyke." We went back to the supply depot, and he told that sergeant what he could do with that statement of charges! Lt. Nix was a wonderful leader, always looking out for his crew.

By this time, we were all beginning to feel the mental strain and physical effects of combat flying. We were usually notified the day before each bombing mission, making sleep that night difficult due to anxious thoughts about where we might be going and how well defended the target area might be. That nervous feeling remained with me until the first enemy fighters were sighted or the anti-aircraft shells began to explode around us. As I got caught up in the action, my butterflies would disappear.

Most men smoked cigarettes at the time. The Army rationed each soldier seven packs of cigarettes a week while we were in Italy. Five of the packs were good quality brands like Lucky Strike and Camel, but the other two packs were cheap brands like Fleetwood and Chelsea that smoked like hay. Since Army meals were not very good, we started trading the bad cigarettes with the local boys in return for eggs. This arrangement worked for a few weeks until the boys somehow got a taste of the better American brands and figured out we were unloading the cheap ones on them. When we tried to give them packs of Fleetwood or Chelsea in return for the eggs, the Italian kids would protest, "No! No! Lucky Strike!"

One of our next targets was the Münchendorf Airdrome on May 24, 1944. On this mission, we were loaded with small fragmentation bombs weighing about twenty pounds each. The bombs were made of a series of small rings that would break into even smaller pieces when they exploded, sending shrapnel over a large area.

All bombs, whether large or small, were equipped with a detonator pin on its nose and fins on the rear to make it fall straight. A small propeller covered the detonator pin. When bombs were loaded onto the plane, a small wire was inserted through a hole in the propeller blade and attached to the bomb racks. When the bombs were released, the wire pulled out of the propeller, allowing it to spin off, exposing the detonator pin and allowing it to explode upon impact.

During this mission, Lt. Nix called me up to the flight deck to discuss a minor mechanical problem. To get to the flight deck from my waist gun position, I had to walk over a catwalk less than one foot wide between the bomb bay racks. On my way over, I caught sight of a small fragmentation bomb that had broken loose from the cluster and was rolling around on the bomb bay doors. Due to the close formation we were flying in, there was a great deal of side slippage, causing this bomb to roll back and forth.

I told Lt. Nix about our issue and we discussed possible ways to safely dispose of the bomb. On most bombers, the bomb bay doors opened down and outward, but on a B-24, they rolled up the side of the aircraft. We feared that if we simply opened the bomb bay doors, the small propeller on this bomb might rotate off, exposing the detonator pin and putting us all in immediate danger. We decided the best solution would be for me to return to the catwalk and pick up the bomb. Lt. Nix would open the bomb bay doors and give me a signal when it was okay to let it go.

With the bomb in my hands, I crouched on this very narrow catwalk above the bay doors, which were cracked open about six inches. There was no intercom jack in this section of the plane, so I waited for the hand signal. While I was in no personal danger holding this weapon, I felt uneasy with it cradled in my arms. It seemed like Lt. Nix was taking forever to give me the signal, and it was getting pretty breezy back there on the catwalk above open bomb bay doors 20,000 feet in the air. Adding to my anxiety was the fact that I was not wearing a parachute because the catwalk was so narrow, and my knowledge that the bomb bay doors a few feet below supported only 100 pounds of weight. Finally, after what seemed like a lifetime, Lt. Nix signaled for me to let it go.

When I returned to the flight deck, I asked Lt. Nix why he had waited so long before giving me the signal. He explained that our navigator saw we were flying over a small village and feared the bomb might hit this town if we let it go too soon. Here we were, part of a large bomber group loaded with fragmentation bombs intended to destroy a German airfield, yet we were concerned about dropping a single bomb on a small village we knew nothing about. In spite of the calloused feeling we were developing for the value of life during war, I guess we could still show compassion toward innocent people living in a small, obscure village somewhere in Europe.

CHAPTER TWELVE

Soldiers Aren't Supposed to Cry

Whenever extensive repairs were made to a plane, it had to be fully checked out before it went on a mission again. Checking how well the aircraft and engines performed at high altitudes after repairs fell on Lt. Nix and me. This was a monotonous task but a necessary one to prevent a crew from taking a faulty plane out on a mission.

On the morning of June 9, 1944, our crew assembled at the aircraft where Lt. Nix informed us that our target that day was a rail yard in Munich, as well-defended a city as any we had previously bombed. Lt. Nix asked the crew to vote on what we should do if we sustained heavy damage. Did we want to try to make it back to our base or should we head for Switzerland, a neutral country about one hundred miles away?

It was common to hear crewmen talk about landing in or bailing out over Switzerland as the easy way out of the war. Many crews did just that. Records indicate that a total of eighty-one crews landed or crashed there during the war. On March 18, 1944 alone, twelve B-24 crews landed in that country. Due to either combat fatigue or just being tired of facing what seemed to be certain death day in and day out, some decided to end their flying and fighting for the duration of the war. I am not being critical of these men or questioning their actions in any way. Under the circumstances, it's understandable that the constant danger and fear for one's life became too much for some.

The other eight guys in our crew told Lt. Nix they wanted to "head for Switzerland." Naturally, Archie joked, "I wouldn't mind chasing some Swiss gal up and down the Alps." But I voted that we should try to make it back to our base. I knew if we landed in Switzerland, our crew would be interred for the duration of the war, and I was eager to get home.

On that particular day, our plane received only minor damage. Despite what the other men had voted, I am certain we would have tried to return to our base had we acquired even more damage.

I never envied the duties of the pilot and co-pilot on a bombing mission. On the final bomb run, the entire formation had to move closer together to produce a more concentrated bomb drop. During tight formation flying, the pilot and co-pilot would alternate taking the controls every few minutes. They often had to react very quickly when anti-aircraft shells exploded near the plane, causing it to move violently in an unexpected direction. Personally, I never saw it happen over a target, but it was reported that a few planes did collide in mid-air during these types of maneuvers.

Also, as enemy fighters attacked our formation, those of us assigned to gunner positions possessed a means of defense and retaliation. But the pilot and co-pilot could only fly the aircraft and observe the action. Both our pilot, Lt. Nix, and co-pilot, Lt. Fields, were great men who performed their duties with excellence. I always considered them a couple of "real cool dudes."

On many missions, I was called to the flight deck to discuss mechanical problems that developed due to damage to our aircraft. Both of these men usually had beads of perspiration on their faces despite outside temperatures at twenty degrees below zero. The physical and mental strain experienced by these two men while flying in close formation and under enemy fire is beyond description.

On one of our missions, a plane from our squadron was hit over the target and went out of control. As the plane was going down, I observed three men (navigator, bombardier, and nose gunner) bail out of the nose section. The pilot, Lt. Hillman, regained control of his plane and regrouped with our formation. Even though he told us later that he didn't expect to recover, he said he didn't understand why his men bailed out. After this mission, and this incident, Lt. Hillman was immediately sent back to the States due to concerns about his emotional condition.

Eventually, the stress became too much for our pilot. Sometime after our second raid on Ploesti, Lt. Nix was relieved of his duties due to excessive fatigue. We could all see its effect on him in his actions and his demeanor. This easy-going Texan's whole character had changed over the course of our time together. The man who never had a harsh word for any member of the crew at the start of his service sometimes came down overly hard on men for minor details he would have laughed off before. Our flight surgeon questioned me about his condition, and I spoke what I believed to be the truth. Lt. Nix was sent home and our co-pilot, Lt. Fields, took over as command pilot.

With Lt. Nix's departure, another member of our original crew was now gone. Needless to say, it was a very sad farewell. They say soldiers aren't supposed to cry, but many did on the occasion of his leaving.

CHAPTER THIRTEEN

Close Calls

Taking off was the most critical moment of every mission due to the heavy bomb load, a fuel supply filled to capacity, and a short runway. Planes assembled according to their position in the flying formation and took off in 30- to 45-second intervals. We almost always encountered turbulence from the plane taking off ahead of us. After one plane took off, the next would taxi into position. With propellers set to full pitch, flaps down to create more lift, and the engine set at full throttle, we waited for our signal from the timer. At that point, the brakes were released and off we would go.

I do not recall the target on our first mission with Lt. Fields as command pilot, but I remember the take-off well. The plane ahead of us crashed at the end of the runway because its landing gear had collapsed just prior to take-off. Fortunately, it did not catch fire and everyone escaped unharmed. This was the same plane we had been flying on a mission to Budapest when Lt. Bush was killed. We had brought it back heavily damaged that day, and this was to be its first mission after it had been repaired. That aircraft never flew again, but it did serve as a source for replacement parts.

With this wreckage lying at the far end of the runway, the flight command center directed us to taxi to the opposite end for take-off in the opposite direction — downwind, which was typically a no-no. I called out our air speed as we headed down the runway. We needed to reach about 120 to 130 miles per hour to safely become airborne, but as we neared the olive grove at the end of the runway, we had reached only 110. This was too slow for a successful take-off, but our only option was to try to become airborne anyway. I yelled to Lt. Fields, "Get her up!" We lifted off the ground, and he immediately retracted the landing gear to lessen the drag on the plane.

How we cleared the olive trees and remained airborne, I'll never know. Our old B-24 began to shake and shudder as it struggled to stay above the trees. I expected our plane to stall out and crash into the tree tops at any moment. There is not much chance for survival in a bomber carrying a full bomb load. But Lt. Fields managed to gain the altitude we needed. His skill as a pilot got us through a tough situation caused by the short-ened runway and downwind take-off.

On each mission, we were given a primary target, a secondary target, and the target of last resort. More than once, we were unable to see a target due to overcast skies. Because it was dangerous to land with a full payload, we would dump our bombs in the ocean and return to base with no mission to our credit, having accomplished absolutely nothing.

On one mission, after flying over what seemed to be half the continent of Europe, our group leader decided to bomb the target of last resort because the first two were completely invisible due to heavy cloud cover. As we approached the harbor over Genoa on the final bomb run, there were a few bursts of flak, and Major Reid put the entire formation into a very tight left turn. Our plane was on the extreme inside of this turn, so in order to stay in formation, our pilot was forced to reduce speed.

I was standing by the opening at the right waist gun position when our plane slipped violently in the oppo-site direction as our pilot overcompensated with the controls. The spent shell casings from firing at enemy fighters were lying on the floor, and I must have slipped on them. As our plane turned hard to the left, I lost my balance and fell out the opening on the right side of the fuselage. I grabbed hold of the gun sight that stood about an inch high at the end of the barrel and held on for dear life. I wasn't wearing a parachute, only the harness one could be snapped onto if needed. Corporal Mongeon, who was standing on the left side waist gun, saw that I was in trouble, hanging out the window from my waist up. He took hold of my harness and yanked me safely back into the plane. It was a close call … too close for comfort.

Several planes lost control and dropped out of formation. One of these was Crew #7 piloted by Lt. Desperock, considered to be one of the hottest pilots in our squadron. When last seen, we estimated his altitude to be about 5,000 feet, a drop of 15,000 feet. Large bombers like the B-24 did not recover easily from a stall, but he seemed to have his under control. However, we never saw those men again. Alone and away from the rest of the formation, Lt. Desperock's crew was probably attacked by enemy fighters as they attempted to return to our base.

To my knowledge, this was the first time our group had been led by Major Reid. Some said he was given the honor of leading the group because of his rank. I'm sure his leadership capabilities were questioned by many of the crews that day. We returned to base after dumping our bomb loads in the ocean.

On the days we were not scheduled to fly, we would rush out to the runway when we heard the planes returning to watch them land. Bombers circled the base waiting their turn. Planes with casualties on board would fire a flare pistol giving them priority to land first. If a plane was badly damaged but had no crew members with injuries, they would usually land last because of the possibility of crashing and preventing the other planes from being able to land. Ambulances and fire trucks were always present at landings.

One day, a returning plane could not lower its flaps and had no brakes because the hydraulic system had been shot away. Because it was coming in at a high rate of speed with no brakes or flaps, this crew received permission to bail out over an area a short distance from the base. The pilot set the plane on auto pilot, and the entire crew bailed out. A few of us drove an Army truck to pick up the crew. We found one of them hanging in a tree in his parachute harness. As the plane headed toward the Adriatic Sea, a couple of our fighters were sent to shoot it down.

On a different day, when I was not scheduled to fly, a terrible accident occurred at our base. Archie and I were headed to the mess hall for dinner when we stopped to watch the planes returning from a mission. They were circling the base about 500 feet off the ground when one plane cut off the entire tail section of another with its left propeller. The plane with the damaged tail dropped straight down nose first and exploded on impact. The other plane went into a long glide, crashing near the area where we parked our planes. This plane caught fire and one crew member was pulled from the burning wreckage by a mechanic. He suffered a broken back in the crash. A total of twenty men were lost in this tragic accident. One of the casualties of this incident was Lt. Jackson, the pilot who made the trip overseas with our crew.

I was always anxious to receive a letter from home. It was through these letters from family that I learned Mom's condition was getting worse. I flew every mission I could, substituting on other crews, hoping I could finish my missions and get home in time to see her again. I had gotten about eight missions ahead of my crew, but I paid the price for pushing myself too hard. I was grounded due to illness for almost two weeks in the middle of June 1944. My crewmates told me I had been admitted to the hospital. I don't remember that.

CHAPTER FOURTEEN

War Is a Sad Experience

During the last three weeks of June of 1944, our group suffered staggering losses at a rate that exceeded replacements. Replacement crews were arriving in new airplanes covered in bright, shiny aluminum skins instead the usual drab green paint. Sadly, we hardly got to know some of the new crew members before they were lost on a mission.

The pilot on one replacement crew that arrived was Lt. Jones. He arrived in a new silver B-24 with "Emperor Jones" painted under the cockpit window. I thought,

"This guy is …" They often split up these new crews, so one day he flew as our co-pilot. Before his first mission with us, I told him there was a steel helmet behind his seat to wear when we got over our target.

"I never wear them," he said. Apparently, he had never seen a pop of flak in his life.

Before take-off that day, our top turret gunner, Sgt. Barrett, had to piss, so he used that helmet. When we needed to urinate when airborne, there was a tube with a little funnel at the top that ran out of the airplane. But for the second or third guy who had to pee, the tube would be blocked because at 20,000 feet the temperature in the airplane was forty degrees below zero, so it didn't take long for anything to freeze. That is exactly what happened to Barrett's deposit in the helmet — it froze when we reached a high altitude. When the flak started popping near the target, Jones grabbed his helmet and placed it on his head. The warmth from his head slowly melted its contents, which dribbled down Jones' face while Barrett sat there laughing his butt off.

My official records indicate that the mission on June 25, 1944 to Avignon lasted only ten minutes longer than the raid on Ploesti, which had been almost eight hours. But I recall this mission lasting over ten hours. Several of the planes from our group were forced to land at the Island of Corsica because their fuel supply was too low to make it back to our home base. They arrived the next day after refueling.

On June 26, 1944, radio operator Corporal Mongeon and I were grounded by the flight surgeon due to severe colds. Crew members were not allowed to fly if we had head colds because our inner ears could be damaged. Sgt. Beland, who I had filled in for when he was wounded, was flying in my place because he wanted to catch up to his crew in missions flown. At this time, my crewmates had completed nearly forty missions, and I was still eight missions ahead of them.

That afternoon, Sgt. Nielsen and I stood near the flight line waiting for the crews to return. Their mission that day was to a refinery at Moosbierbaum, Austria. It was expected to be an easy mission, what we called a "milk run." When we didn't see my crew's plane ("Old #233"), I asked some of the returning crews if they knew what happened. They told me my crew had been shot down over Hungary. Other crews always kept a close eye on how many parachutes they counted coming out of any plane that was going down. They told me they saw all ten. Still, I had no way of knowing if the crew members were safe at this point. I sat in disbelief at the spot where our plane usually parked. It was pretty devastating!

Two hours later, the chaplain and someone from the Red Cross came to my tent and told me that Mom had died earlier that day. I had wanted to return home in time to see her, but it was not to be. I remember them expressing their concern not only for the death of my mother and the loss of my crew, but also for me.

That day, I felt like the whole world was crashing in on me! I had tried to complete my fifty missions as quickly as possible so I could see Mom before she died. But instead, I had gotten myself in a run-down condition, and was grounded and unable to get home in time.

On July 3, I flew my final mission to Malaxa. I don't remember what crew I was with that day. I might have been assigned to a replacement crew that had never been in combat before; sometimes an experienced person was placed with a new crew. Or I might have been placed with members of various crews who had suffered losses. I really don't recall.

My safe return to the base meant I had now completed my 50th mission, an accomplishment I never thought possible given the odds. I believe I was the first airman in our squadron to reach this goal.

I have often been asked, "Which was the worst mission: the first or last?" I can assure you that the last one created the most anxiety because I knew that when that mission was completed, I finally would be done.

Upon landing, someone told commanding officer Colonel Steed I had completed my missions. He came out to the aircraft to congratulate me while a photographer, who was also responsible for public relations, took my picture. Colonel Steed told the photographer not to send the photo to my hometown newspaper yet because I might need to fly more missions due to the heavy losses our group had suffered. My heart sunk and I thought to myself, "Oh man!" What an awful feeling — to think I had finished my missions only to have Colonel Steed say more might be required.

That night, alone in my tent, I began to question how much more I could endure. I had lost more than forty pounds since I left California. I must have been skin and bones at the time. But it was not just my physical condition that was a problem. With all that had happened — the death of my mother, the loss of so many friends, the constant stress of war — my mental condition had worsened.

I didn't know it at the time, but on that day only two of the eight planes from our squadron that went up that day returned. I imagine the heavy losses were fresh in Colonel Steed's mind, which is why he made the comment about me possibly needing to fly more missions. I wish he would have shared this information because I might have handled it better.

On July 5, 1944, I was examined by the flight surgeon who signed a statement certifying that I was in "an anxious state, acute, resulting from prolonged duty." His statement further stated that I was "reduced in operational efficiency as to affect the efficiency of the organization" but that I would be "physically rehabilitated within a 90-day period." I was ordered to be returned to the United States "on detached service." I must have been in pretty bad shape.

The day before I left my base, I walked out to the flight line after the crews returned from a mission to say goodbye to Sgt. Nielsen and Corporal Inman. I had grown very close to these men while I was a flight engineer. They were both excellent mechanics, as were so many of the other maintenance personnel on the base. These men would work well into the night and still be at the aircraft in the morning before take-off time to review repairs and check engine performance. On many occasions, a plane would return from a mission so badly damaged it seemed it would never fly again. But due to the excellent work performed by our maintenance personnel, it would soon be ready for missions.

Later that evening, I said my goodbyes to some of the men who had been with us from the beginning. I don't think there were any complete crews remaining of the original twenty-two that left the states together. I walked to the spot where my plane used to park and there stood a new, shiny silver B-24.

"What a beautiful ship," I said to Sgt. Nielsen.

With tears in his eyes, he replied, "Dyke, it just isn't the same. There will never be another crew like you guys were."

We sat for a long time in the shade of the new aircraft, sharing our thoughts about the war and our feelings about the men we had become so close to, many who were no longer with us. I asked Nielsen to destroy the letters I had given him to mail to my parents and Alice in case I did not return from a mission. In one of them I had written to her, "Don't mourn for me. Find yourself another man."

On the day before I left the base, I saw Pvt. McHenry and Sparky, two men who had refused to fly. McHenry was picking up spent cigarette butts. Both men were still doing menial tasks around the base. Neither had any friends. They lived together in a tent by themselves. I'm sure this was ordered by superior officers to isolate and humiliate them. One night, someone acquired some yellow paint and threw it on their tent. Both were shunned by almost everyone. Even the replacement crews soon learned the story behind these two individuals. Sometimes I felt sorry for them.

Shakespeare wrote, "Cowards die many times before their deaths. The valiant never taste of death but once." I believe I would rather have died in combat than suffer the humiliation these men endured.

On July 6, I received orders to pack my bags. I would be taken by truck to Naples where I would board a victory ship for my voyage to the United States. I cannot find words to express my feelings that day as our truck drove away from the base that had been my home for less than five months. There had been so many tragedies; so many of my old friends were no longer around. I was happy it was all over, but a tremendous sadness came over me.

War is a sad experience.

CHAPTER FIFTEEN

A Sight I Will
Never Forget

The night before we left Naples, they showed a movie titled *Up In Arms* starring Danny Kaye and Dinah Shore at an outdoor theater. Halfway through the movie, the air raid sirens sounded, and all lights were immediately turned off. German bombers were taking aim on the Naples harbor. I worried they might sink my transportation home. I shared a foxhole with several other soldiers and watched the American anti-aircraft batteries in action. It looked like a giant fireworks display. It was nice to be on the opposite end of the action for a change.

The next morning, I boarded the USS Henry Gibbins, along with other military personnel and 982 Jewish refugees from 18 different countries, for my voyage home. These would be the only European refugees brought to our country by the government during the war. There was resistance in the States to accepting refugees due to the isolationist sentiment left over from WWI and concerns regarding domestic security.*

German submarines remained active in the Atlantic at this point in the war, so our ship joined a convoy of ten other ships escorted by eight Navy cruisers and destroyers for protection.

Near dusk one evening, while still in the Mediterranean Sea, enemy aircraft were spotted. An alarm was sounded and the ships in the convoy sent out a smoke screen. Most of us were below deck either reading or sleeping. Since it was quite warm this time of year, all the hatches were open and smoke poured into the deck below. It was scary but none of the ships in the convoy suffered any damage.

When we first boarded the ship, we were given orders that every able-bodied soldier was required to volunteer for some type of work during the voyage. Almost all of the other troops on the ship were headed home permanently, but I only had a single sheet of paper placing me on detached service from my unit for ninety days before I would have to return. The idea of having to go back into combat left me feeling bitter toward the Army at this time. So when I boarded that ship, I decided I was not going to volunteer for anything. My plan worked for the first three days. But after we passed through the Straits of Gibraltar, an officer came up to me while I was lying in my hammock down in the hole reading a book and asked, "Soldier, what are you doing on this ship?"

He scared the daylights out of me because I didn't hear him walk up. "Nothing, sir," I replied.

He said, "Follow me," and took me down to the galley, where I was assigned to work in the kitchen, mainly as a dish washer. This actually turned out to be a pretty good deal because the galley workers ate the best of food whenever they wanted. The merchant marine in charge told us, "Everybody else on this ship eats two meals a day. When they're done eating, we eat. But we don't eat what they eat." I lived like a king and even gained a few pounds on the voyage home.

The refugees on board were certainly to be pitied. Some appeared to be in terrible physical condition. I assume many had been liberated from a concentration camp in Northern Italy by Allied troops. These refugees were confined to a separate part of the ship, but I saw many while serving their meals. I will never forget the sight of those people as long as I live. They were walking skeletons.

We were instructed not to put too much food on their trays because their digestive systems could not handle it. One day, while serving mashed potatoes from a huge vat, I put a single ice cream scoopful on an old Jewish guy's tray. He angrily pointed at it, pleading for more.

Refusing that poor man another scoop of potatoes was one of the hardest things I ever had to do.

One night on deck, I struck up a conversation with the soldier standing next to me. I learned he was a fighter pilot who had crashed during one of his missions. His face was disfigured and badly burned. His main concern about going back home was how his wife would react when she first saw him again. We spent many nights on the deck, leaning against the rail, sharing our experiences. Sad to say, I can't recall his name now.

I also shared discussions about combat experiences with several infantry men on board. Many told me they didn't see how we, the air crews, had the guts to fly. But I certainly would not have traded places with them. As I read stories of the battles they fought, I believe the infantry men, the "dog face" or "foot soldier" as they were called, were the key to winning the war. They were the first troops to set foot on mainland Europe on D-Day, June 6, 1944. Along with the Marines who took back island after island from the Japanese in the Pacific Theater, I believe these were the real heroes of World War II.

During our voyage home, the ocean appeared as a continuous series of small ripples. Merchant marine personnel said they had never seen the Atlantic so smooth. Near the end of July, our convoy broke apart as ships headed to different American ports. New York City was our final destination because the refugees on board were required to go to Ellis Island for processing. As we entered the New York Harbor on August 3, 1944, we passed by the Statue of Liberty, the enduring symbol of American freedom. It is a sight I will never forget.

*Chapter Note:

The story of these refugees and their voyage to the United States and settlement in Oswego, New York is told by Ruth Gruber in her book *Haven: The Dramatic Story of 1,000 World War II Refugees and How They Came to America* (2010).

CHAPTER SIXTEEN

Adjusting to Stateside

After we docked in New York, Red Cross workers greeted us with fresh milk and a chocolate candy bar. Even though I had eaten well on the way home on the victory ship, I arrived in New York weighing only 125 pounds. When I left California for overseas seven months earlier, I had weighed 168 pounds.

I boarded a train to Atlantic City for processing. During a short stay at the Air Force redistribution center there, we were given a two-hour lecture on how we should conduct ourselves while on leave. We were told not to give out any information about bombing missions, the number of planes lost on missions, or anything that could possibly benefit the enemy. We were also told to clean up the language we picked up while in the military. The person giving the lecture said, "Don't say, 'Pass the damn grease.' Say, 'Please, pass the butter.'" There were several other examples provided, but they are too foul to put in writing.

From New Jersey, I was sent to Fort Sheridan in Illinois to receive new clothing and the necessary papers for my leave. I arrived in Kankakee around 6:30 in the evening and was greeted by Pa, my sister Millie, my brother Harry, and my brother Neil and his wife Myrtle. I was given twenty-three wonderful days at home before reporting to Miami Beach, Florida.

I had been home for three days before I contacted Alice. I feared that the feelings we expressed for each other through our correspondence would not hold true when we saw each other in person. Was the love we expressed for each other in our letters emotions brought on by the war? Or was it for real? How two people can fall in love through letters I'll never know, but it happened.

While I was home on leave, there were times when things became a little tense between Millie and me. An elderly person in our community had passed away, and I evidently didn't show enough remorse for Millie's liking. She said, "Ralph, you are as hard as nails." Her comment hurt somewhat, and maybe it was true. But I found it difficult to express sorrow for an older person who passed away after I had seen so many young men die who never had a chance to live a full life.

Life at home quickly became boring. Dad was an avid reader and my sister Millie was always busy, so I had no one to talk to. Alice was still in nursing training and was on duty several nights of the week. The quietness drove me up a wall. Sometimes, late in the evening, I would drive to St. Anne just to find someone to talk to. I know that this concerned my dad, but being away from Army life was a difficult adjustment.

I had the home addresses of the guys in my crew, and I knew that our bombardier, Lt. Busse, was from Chicago. My brother Neil knew his way around Chicago, so he offered to drive Pa and me there to see Busse's wife. I wanted to tell her what I knew about the crew's last mission. I remember her coming to the door holding their little baby who was born while her husband was overseas.

When my leave was over, I traveled to Miami Beach for another thirty days of R&R. Here, I stayed in a lovely hotel on the beach with no duties. The only thing required of me was to check the bulletin board in the hotel lobby each day for dental or doctor appointments. Here, I also saw the end of the movie *Up in Arms* that the German bombers had so rudely interrupted in Naples. I lived like royalty. Was this the Army?

Sometime between my departure from Italy and my arrival in Miami Beach, my records were changed and I found out I would not have to return to my unit in Europe. For this, I was very thankful.

From Miami, I was sent to Charleston Air Base in South Carolina. My duties included mechanical work on B-24s. I also served as an instructor for new crews training for combat. One day, I was assigned to fly as a flight engineer with an 8th Air Force bomber pilot had completed his tour of duty in England. A civilian pilot was going to check him out to see if he was qualified to be an instruction pilot. I don't know why they had to have a guy who flew 35 missions over Europe checked out to be an instructor. Anyhow, during our flight, the civilian pilot told the returnee pilot to take our B-24 up to 10,000 feet and stall it out. He put the plane in a stall and it dropped one way and then the other way until the 8th Air Force pilot pulled it out of the stall at around 9,000 feet.

"That wasn't good enough," the civilian pilot said. "Take this thing back up to 10,000 feet and do it again."

When we got to that altitude, the bomber pilot stalled it out again. He kicked the rudder pedal, and the plane swung in one direction and then violently in the other direction; then down we went into a steep dive. The airspeed indictor went past the red line, and I was sure I was going to die. He pulled it out at about 2,500 feet. When we landed, he looked over at the civilian instructor and asked, "Was that good enough?"

I said to the civilian pilot, "I will never fly with you again."

"What's the matter? Are you chicken?" he replied.

"I didn't fly over half the continent of Europe getting my butt shot off to come back to the United States to get killed flying with a jackass like you," I said. If he had been an officer in the Air Force I would have kept my mouth shut. But he was a civilian so he couldn't do anything to me.

After two months at Charleston, I was sent to Wichita Falls, Texas, and then on to Tarrant Field in Fort Worth, Texas, to serve as a flight engineer with instructor pilots. When there was no experienced instructor pilot available, I took part in take-offs and landings with pilots who had never flown an airplane the size of a B-24 before. We had a lot of close calls.

During these practice flights, I stood between two armored plates that separated the cockpit from the back of the plane. On one landing, the pilot in training dropped our plane down like a rock, so hard our landing gear collapsed and we skidded down the runway. I was thrown into one of the armored plates, banging my shoulder very hard. It was the worst landing I had ever experienced.

My shoulder bothered me for days, so I made a visit to the flight surgeon. After examining my injury, he said, "You're an overseas returnee. What are you doing flying with these kids? You're going to get yourself killed! Do you want me to ground you?"

"Yes, sir," I said. The flight surgeon changed my flight records to read "no longer fit for flying status."

After that, I was made a skeet instructor. I really enjoyed competing with the officers who practiced at the range, but some of these men had never held a shotgun before and had little knowledge of its danger at close range. Sometimes I worried that this assignment might be more dangerous than flying.

After spending about two months at Fort Worth, I began to tire of the same old routine. I heard there were vacancies at Langley Field, Virginia, and signed up for a transfer. Langley Field was a proving ground for new engines and aircraft, so I thought it would be an interesting place to be, and I would learn something. Two other returnees I had never met before also signed up for this transfer. They were John Hiten from Kentucky and Bill Yendell from New York.

Upon arriving at Langley Field, we were assigned our barracks and told to report to a lieutenant whose name I can't recall. We reported at 9:00 in the morning and he wasn't in his office, so we went back to the barracks. The next few days the same thing happened. On the fifth day, he was in his office and his first statement to us was, "Well, if it isn't the fast firing trio!" He then proceeded to give us a good butt chewing.

Yendell was from New York and he didn't take grief from anybody. "It must be nice to have a job where you're only in your office one day in five," he said. Oh, the shit hit the fan! When the lieutenant's aid started to yell at us, Yendell said to him, "Why don't you shut up! I've got more time in the chow line than you've got in the Army."

We were ordered to report to Captain Wilson, a WWI veteran who had made the Army his career and probably attained that rank through his many years in service. Captain Wilson was in charge of the area that supplied coal to heat the barracks, so our job was to haul coal around. When that task was finished, we would take piles of dumped lumber and sort it into proper stacks.

This was my most carefree time in the service. I took more smoke breaks and had more goof-off time in the four weeks under Captain Wilson's command than in my entire Army career. One of his favorite statements was, "While you are resting, do this or that." One day, I asked Captain Wilson how we could do the task he wanted done while we were resting. He replied, "Oh, you know what I mean." I could never figure him out, and I suppose he thought the same of us. He was a good old boy who probably sympathized with our situation as overseas returnees.

Eventually, three tech sergeants driving a pickup truck and shoveling coal seemed like such a waste of time to me. One day we were coming back from chow, and I saw a sign that read, "Sign up for overseas returnees." I told the other guys, "I don't know about you, but I'm sick of this. I'm going in there to sign up to go back overseas."

Around April 1, 1945, orders arrived transferring me to Tyndall Field in Panama City, Florida. I was given twenty-one days to report, so I came home for a few days. During this leave, President Roosevelt died at his winter retreat in Georgia. What a sad day for our nation!

I believe that two of the greatest men who lived during my lifetime were President Franklin Roosevelt and British Prime Minister Winston Churchill. The feeling of the American people at the beginning of Germany's rise to power was to remain neutral. Many recalled WWI and did not want to become involved in another war to free Europe. President Roosevelt's foresight and the military buildup he urged in the late 1930s saved this from becoming a greater conflict. It saddens me to think that the man who led this nation through some of this world's darkest days would not live to see the end of the war.

While home on leave, Alice and I became engaged. I asked my sister-in-law Myrtle to help me pick out an engagement ring. I must have been rather confident of Alice's answer since I bought the ring before the proposal. I sure am happy she accepted. Why she agreed to become my wife is something I still find hard to understand. I had nothing of value to offer except my everlasting love. I'm certain that in her quiet way, Alice helped me overcome some of the anxieties that still remained from the war. What a wonderful person!

CHAPTER SEVENTEEN

A Birthday Gift for Alice

On April 20, 1945, I reported to Tyndall Field to begin training on the A-26, which was used strictly for low-level bombing. It was one of the hottest twin engine bombers the Air Force had at this time. It held three people: a pilot, co-pilot, and a gunner in the back. I had only one ride on an A-26, but what a plane! Oh, man, it flew!

Why I volunteered to go back into combat I'll never know. It may have been from my current boredom or the earlier excitement of seeing another part of the world. But when I look back on it now, it was a stupid idea. Fortunately, after I had been at Tyndall Field for about a month, Germany surrendered, ending the war in Europe. Hitler committed suicide, and Mussolini was taken by his people to be hanged by his feet to die. I was in a barracks with six guys when an announcement came over the PA system: "The war in Europe is over. All overseas returnees report to Theater Two tomorrow morning at 9:00." They told us we would not be returning to combat.

I was to be transferred again, so the Army gave me three choices for reassignment: Chanute Field in Illinois; Mitchell Field in New York; or Tucson, Arizona. I picked Chanute because it was only seventy miles from home. But, typical of the Army, they sent me to Davis Monthan Field in Tucson. I should have been smarter and picked one of the other two because then they might have sent me to Chanute.

In Arizona, I worked as a crew chief in charge of maintenance on B-29 bombers. I was on duty one night from 11:00 to 7:00 in the morning when someone from the flight line shack came out and said, "Hey, Dyke, there's a crippled B-29 coming in." I went outside with a couple flashlights and directed the plane where to park. Out popped this full Colonel who had that "bird" (eagle insignia) perched on his shoulder signifying his high rank. He asked me to check out the engine. The first thing we were taught to do was pull the oil screen, which I found was full of metal filings.

"Sir, you won't be able to take off with that engine," I said. "It's dead."

"Well, I want a new engine," he demanded.

"Sir, I'm not authorized to put a new engine on your plane," I replied.

"Who the hell is?" he asked. He was irate. I told him I was just following Army regulations and he had to talk to the captain in the flight shack. Afterward, he came out stomping and cussing. "I'm at a B-29 base and I can't even get an engine." I guess he had to take it out on somebody. Finally, someone with authority ordered an engine to be pulled off another B-29 and put on his plane.

In August 1945, two atomic bombs were dropped on Japan, completely destroying Nagasaki and Hiroshima. Japan surrendered, and the atomic age was born. How fortunate it was that the Unites States was the first nation to develop such power. I dread to think what our world would be like now had one of our enemies developed it first.

The end of the war started the giant task of discharging most of the military personnel from their service. The Army used a point system to determine if a soldier was eligible for discharge. I had enough points but would have to wait until the separation center nearest to my home at Fort Sheridan, Illinois, was able to process my discharge. But then they told me that if I had my own transportation from Tucson, I could be discharged immediately. I sent Alice a telegram on September 23,

1945, telling her the good news. It read: DARLING WAS DISCHARGED TODAY AND WILL BE HOME NEXT WEEK WILL CELEBRATE YOUR BIRTHDAY WILL SEND ANOTHER LATER ALL MY LOVE. RALPH.

For our transportation home, a guy named Findley from Illinois, three guys from Michigan, and I pitched in and bought a 1936 Nash for $250. We agreed to each take two-hour shifts behind the wheel and drive straight home from Tucson. Late on the first day, we blew a front tire while I was driving. We changed the tire and then creeped across the desert at about 30 miles per hour because we didn't dare drive too fast in the middle of nowhere with only four good tires and no spare. When we arrived in Albuquerque, we pulled into a gas station and asked if they had any tires. "Yes. 150 bucks," the attendant said. A taxi driver was sitting there, and he said to us, "Follow me out of town. I'll get you a tire." He took us to a junk yard and a guy there sold us two good tires for half the price that the gas station wanted.

On October 1, I updated Alice on my progress home via another telegram sent to St. Mary's Hospital where she was in training. DARLING AM ON WAY HOME NEAR OKLAHOMA CITY SHOULD BE HOME BY FRIDAY WILL SEE YOU THEN ALL MY LOVE. RALPH.

By the time we reached Kansas City, the engine on the Nash started to knock pretty bad, so we decided we had better sell it. We saw a policeman and asked him where we could find a used car dealer in town. He pointed us to one a couple blocks away. We told the salesman we had just arrived at home and wanted to sell our car. A train passed by at the very moment he started it and he couldn't hear the knock. He gave us $125 for the car, so it cost each of us 25 bucks to get from Tucson to Kansas City.

We boarded a bus and Findley got off in Lexington, a town in central Illinois. He said, "Dyke, come home with me. My mom will cook us noon dinner." After a wonderful meal, his father drove me back to Route 66. I stuck out my thumb, and a man driving a 1942 Pontiac (the last year they made new cars) picked me up, "Where are you going, soldier?"

"Kankakee," I said.

"I'm going as far as Dwight. I'll drop you off there."

In Dwight, I got out at the stop sign at the intersection of routes 66 and 17, carried my bag across the street, and a semi-truck came by. "Where are you going, soldier?"

"Kankakee."

"Hop in, I'm heading there."

He dropped me off at the Serve Rite, a little burger and ice cream place on Court Street in Kankakee. My cousin, Sadie Lumpkes, was there and she gave me a ride. Alice had told me all she wanted for her birthday was my discharge papers. I was home with them that very day, October 5, 1945.

CHAPTER EIGHTEEN

A Bouquet of Lilies

I began farming with my dad in the spring of 1946. Alice and I were married on January 23, 1947. I cannot praise my wife enough for being the kind, gentle person she is. I'm sure that at times it was not easy to be married to a guy whose post-war nerves were on edge.

To our surprise, Lt. Busse and his wife attended the wedding. We probably sent an invitation to his Chicago address without knowing if he had returned from the war. I think that is the first time I learned that my crew had survived being shot down and had been interred in a prison of war camp in Hungary for the remainder of the war. At our reception, I introduced Lt. Busse and his wife to friends and family. Later, Busse said to me, "I never felt comfortable going on a mission without you as flight engineer." He also told Pa, "Your son was the bravest man I ever saw."

I lost track of Busse and never connected with any of the other members of my crew after that. I guess we got busy making a living and raising our children. Alice and I bought our first farm in 1951 and lived there until 1962, when we purchased the farm we now own. A turning point came in 1957 when ten inches of rain in one night destroyed our gladiolus crop. Farm payments had to be made and children still had to be fed, so Alice returned to work as a nurse, and I became employed at Armstrong Cork Company until my retirement in 1988.

A few years after I retired, I played golf with a former St. Anne resident, Don Trudeau. He asked if I was a WWII veteran, and I told him I had served with a B-24 bomber crew. He replied that he was also a flight engineer on a B-24 crew based near the small town of Cerignola in Italy. I asked what bomb group he was with, and he stated it was the 456th. I couldn't believe that two people from the same area held the same position in the same bomb group. What are the odds? I found out that Don had arrived in Italy as a member of a replacement crew sometime late in August of 1944. I had already been back in the states a couple months by this time. His plane was shot down on his fifth mission after being hit by flak. He bailed out over Bucharest where his crew was kept hidden by the underground. Later, they returned to their base in Italy, where he flew twenty more missions before the war ended and he returned home to the United States.

Don told me he had never fired a shot at a German enemy fighter. At first I found this hard to believe because our crew often returned to base with our ammunition supply almost gone due to the many German fighters we encountered. But Don explained that when they were sent on missions to bomb German air bases, they destroyed many German aircraft because their planes were unable to take off. By that time, the Ploesti oil fields and refineries had been destroyed, severely depleting the supply of aviation fuel for the German planes, allowing the skies over Europe to be dominated by the American and British Air Forces.

My chance conversation with Don helped me see that the early missions my crew had flown played a major role in bringing the war to an end. Our repeated bombing of oil fields, factories, and air fields ended Germany's ability to support their war machine. It felt good to realize this.

I thought about the guys from my crew, particularly navigator Lt. Bush, who was killed on an early mission over Budapest. For years, I had thought I should look up his kin. I remembered that he was from Ottumwa, Iowa, so after Alice and I had visited our daughter Jan and her family in Iowa, we decided to swing south on our way home to try to find Bush's family.

Alice and I stopped at a gas station in Ottumwa on Friday, November 2, 1990, where we looked through the phonebook to see if there was anyone with the last name "Bush" listed, but there wasn't. We tried the county courthouse, but they either couldn't or wouldn't give me the information. They suggested we go to the Veteran Affairs Office where same thing happened. Finally, someone suggested we check with the local newspaper office.

When I walked into the office of *The Ottumwa Courier*, I was greeted by a reporter sitting at the desk. "What can I do for you?" When I told him the reason we were there, he said, "I want to interview you about the war." "I didn't come here to be interviewed," I said. "I came here to see if I can find the family of Lt. Bush." I told the reporter about our crew and Lt. Bush's death.

"When did this happen?" he asked. I told him Bush was killed on April 3, 1944. He went back into their archives and returned with microfiche of old newspapers. When he showed me a picture from the files, I said, "That's him."

There was a woman sitting nearby, and she said, "I know Gerald Bush's sister. We go to the same church. I know she's out of town through Saturday." She gave me the sister's name and phone number. I called Ruth Ripley two days later and said, "I am Ralph Dykstra. I knew your brother. I was with him when he was killed."

She told me it was the first time she had talked to anyone from her brother's crew. She shared how a chaplain informed her family that her brother's plane had disintegrated and that the entire crew had been lost. We talked for a while, and I told her I would come see her next spring when we came back to Iowa. Later, as I thought about it more, I decided I shouldn't wait that long.

Alice and I made a special trip back to Ottumwa the next month. Sitting together in her living room, Mrs. Ripley shared with me the letter her brother wrote home the night before his last mission. In it, Lt. Bush said:

"We are leaving soon on a mission from which possibly I won't return, so I want you all to know I am very much in love with you and deeply indebted to all of you. My eyes are full of tears and my heart is heavy. I'm signing off with the Lord's Prayer on my lips. He is going to be with me on this mission and if it is His will that I don't return, it is for a cause well justified."

Mrs. Ripley said the tone of his last letter was more formal than other ones the family received from the easy-going fellow we all knew. She said her brother asked that his watch go to his father, his class ring to his mother, and his savings account used to buy a birthstone ring with a diamond for his girlfriend. The news of his death hit everyone in the family hard, particularly his father who suffered a stroke upon learning of his son's death. A few days later, on Easter Sunday, 1944, his mother received a bouquet of lilies from her dead son.

When asked what prompted me to look up her brother's family after all of these years, I said, "I had misgivings about coming, but I thought if it were my brother, I would want to know how he died. I should have looked for his family years ago, but after the war it was something I wanted to put away, get it out of my mind."

CHAPTER NINETEEN

Beating the Odds

After meeting with Lt. Bush's sister, I started thinking about all the other guys from my crew. I had lost their addresses and didn't know where to begin my search for them or their families. One day, while looking through the 456th Bomb Group Association newsletter, I saw the name of our pilot, Lt. Nix. I obtained his address from the editor and sent a letter to his home in San Bernardino. About ten days later, I received a letter from Mrs. George W. Nix, his wife of 47 years, telling me her husband had passed away from leukemia about six months before my letter arrived. I had begun my search too late.

Later that summer, I started to think about our nose gunner, Archie Hatch. I knew Archie would never leave his home state of Maine, so it was easy to get his number through directory assistance. I called him and we talked for about a half hour. Archie was so excited about us reconnecting, he called me back the next day, and we talked for another half hour or more.

In 1991, our radio operator, Norm Mongeon, and his wife were traveling through the Midwest from their home in Florida. They had stopped at Chanute Air Force Base, which is about seventy smiles south of our home. Norm recalled that I lived in St. Anne, so he looked me up, and I invited them to come to our home. During his visit, we got on the phone together and called Archie; we all agreed to get together with our wives in Maine that fall.

When we got together in September, Archie described the day the crew was shot down returning from their last mission. The group had apparently strayed over Hungary on the way back to the base, and their plane was hit by enemy fire. They bailed out near the town of Papa, Hungary, and became separated on the ground. Archie, who had been wounded in the right foot, was captured immediately by farmers working in the fields where he landed. He spent the remainder of the war recuperating in a prison hospital in Hungary. "I never want to see another bowl of cabbage soup in my life," said Archie, showing he had not lost his sense of humor over the years. Meanwhile, other members of the crew were held as prisoners of war in a camp near Munich, Germany.

A year or so later, I saw our bombardier Paul Busse's name in the newsletter, so I tracked down his phone number and gave him a call. When he answered, I said it was Ralph Dykstra on the line, and he shouted to his wife, "Elvira, get on the phone. It's the guy who saw my son before I did!" Busse told me that Sgt. Beland, who flew in my place on that last mission, was never located after the war. He had received several inquiries from the War Department regarding Beland's condition when last seen. Busse told them he and Beland had landed close to each other after bailing out and that he was okay before they were captured and taken prisoner.

In the fall of 1995, I received a letter in the mail with the name Dudley Fields in the return address. I couldn't open it quickly enough. Inside, he wrote, "Dyke, if you're alive, here's my address." Dudley had found my address through the same 456th Bomb Group newsletter I had used to get Lt. Nix's address. I called Dudley and we talked for a while about our lives since the war and our families. When I learned he was a pilot for United Airlines and occasionally flew to Chicago, I suggested he come down to visit on one of his trips. A few months later he did just that.

We sat at my dining room table and reminisced about our experiences together during the war. Then Dudley shared more about what had happened when they were shot down. As they were coming off the target, they got hit by a German fighter, and the #3 engine caught fire. While the B-24 could fly on three engines, having one of them on fire was very dangerous. After assessing the risk, Dudley ordered the entire crew to bail out.

After hearing Dudley describe their situation that day, I wondered if I could have possibly saved the plane and the crew from bailing had I been on that mission. All B-24s didn't have the same equipment, but our plane had been equipped with a system that could be used in case of an engine fire. A large metal ring with holes in it was located between the propellers and cylinders of each engine. The flight engineer could turn a valve releasing a white powder fire retardant that would extinguish the fire. I don't know if the crew that day wasn't aware of that system or if they just didn't have enough time to deploy it.

Dudley was held captive at various German prisoner of war camps for the next ten months. He told me that toward the end of the war, Hitler gave orders for many of the American POWs to be executed, but German officers disobeyed because they realized the war was about to end. In late April of 1945, Dudley was one of about 50,000 allied troop prisoners of war liberated by the U.S. Third Army. "I can't describe what it felt like when the Swastika came down and was replaced by the American flag," he said with tears in his eyes.

The opportunity to see some of my fellow crewmates again after so many years was truly a blessing. Our reunions offered a chance to reminisce about the people we had met, the places we had seen, and experiences we had shared during wartime. But getting together offered more than that. We learned how fortunate we had each been to be able to return home, to cherish our friends, and to raise our children in the freedom of this great country.

It would have been nice if we had gotten together sooner, but I guess that wasn't meant to be. Perhaps it was better that we waited a few years. The events that had bound us together like brothers were also memories we all felt the need to escape from for a while. Maybe it took that long, more than forty-five years, before the time felt right to revisit those memories and see each other again.

In the fall of 1991, Alice and I drove to Dayton, Ohio, to visit the National Museum of the U.S. Air Force. The occasion marked the dedication of a memorial for the members of the 456th Heavy Bombardment Group who lost their lives during the war. I had been one of the first members of the group to arrive home safely after completing my fifty missions, so this trip had special meaning for me. Even though I was saddened to know that these men did not return home to fully live out their lives, I found comfort in the fact that their sacrifice for the cause of freedom had not been forgotten. I felt honored to have flown over war-torn Europe with them.

At the banquet that evening, Alice and I sat next to a member of the group who shared his personal story of survival with us. Although I never met him while we served in in the same bomb group, I knew his story because I was a witness to it. Bob Gullitt was the lone survivor of that horrible collision between two returning B-24 bombers over our air base in Italy. Twenty men from two crews died in that crash, but Bob was pulled from the burning wreckage despite suffering a broken back. I told Bob I had been there that day. He said that in the more than forty-five years since the accident, I was the first person he met who had witnessed that crash.

Later, I considered the slim odds of meeting the sole survivor of one of the more vivid memories from my wartime experience. But as I thought about it more, I wondered if Bob Gullitt's story of survival and our chance meeting captured much of the essence of our wartime experience — at its core, it was about beating the odds. Bob and I shared more than the memory of a traumatic event. Somehow, by the grace of God, we survived the random nature of war to share our tales with those who care to listen.

I cannot find the right words to express the thoughts that went through my mind during the war, as day after day I faced what seemed to be certain death. But I can honestly say I don't think I ever went on a mission believing I would not come home. Sometimes I think being credited with fifty missions was a great accomplishment, but then I am humbled when I realize it was only through the grace and goodness of Almighty God that my remains are not scattered somewhere over the continent of Europe. It has made me appreciate that every day we are in His care and keeping.

CHAPTER TWENTY

I Never Regretted a Day

Freedom is a priceless possession. I witnessed what happened to war-torn Italy, and it made me appreciate that the battles fought during WWII never reached the continental United States. I remember seeing bombed-out cities, Army tanks, and other damaged war equipment scattered across the Italian countryside, along with American and German aircraft that remained as burned-out wreckage. I saw shoeless children dressed in rags, begging for food. We gave the K-rations we did not eat on our flights to the Italian children, while adults searched the garbage cans outside our mess hall for morsels of food we threw away.

I love this country and the freedom that we, as a people, enjoy. It is easy for me to become misty-eyed at the sight of our flag during parades or while singing our National Anthem. I am proud to have been able to serve my country. My service in that war was my lasting contribution to the country I love so dearly.

On our military bases during WWII, every evening at five o'clock, retreat was held. This involved the lowering of the American flag while "Taps" was played. If anyone happened to be outside their barracks, they would face the direction of the flag and salute it until it was completely lowered and the song had ended. It disturbs me to see the American flag, which has been a symbol of freedom since our nation was founded, being desecrated today. Those who display the American flag as artwork to be walked on or burn it saying they are exercising their constitutional rights are surely not true Americans. I feel that the flag represents the United States of America, the greatest country in the entire world, and it should be honored at all times.

The fight for freedom was very costly. When I think back to the war, it is difficult for me to hold back the tears when I recall that two of my crew members paid the supreme sacrifice, along with over 405,000 young American soldiers who gave their lives that we might have the freedom that we, as a nation, enjoy today. Many others not only carry physical scars from the war, but they hold within themselves invisible wounds that may never heal. José Narosky once said, "In war, there are no unwounded soldiers." I believe that to be true.

Some of the stories I have written here remain vivid in my mind and still haunt me at times. Many other events have become difficult to recall; they are buried deep in the recesses of my mind and will probably only come to full remembrance when I am laid to rest.

I have not written this memoir to set myself up as some sort of hero or glorify my service but to share a bit of American history before it is completely lost. It was worth every sacrifice I made to help free the world of such great oppression. I never regretted a day in the service of my country. Sometimes I still look back at it and wonder, "Why am I here today?"

I thank Almighty God daily for sparing my life. I have shared my life with a wonderful wife and from this union came three wonderful children. My prayer has always been that my children might not experience the ravages of war.

Each of my children married, and I have two daughters-in-law and one son-in-law whom I love as my own. From those marriages, I have been blessed with seven lovely grandchildren and thirteen great-grandchildren, all of whom I love dearly. Now, I offer that same prayer for them: that they never have to experience war.

God has been good to me. I am reminded of what the Psalmist says in the last two verses of the 23rd Psalm: "My cup runneth over. Surely goodness and mercy shall follow me all the days of my life, and I shall dwell in the house of the Lord forever."

My cup, indeed, has been filled to overflowing.

AFTERWORD

"These Are the Skies"

While on a business trip to Italy and Germany a year after I received the original version of my Dad's memoir, I wrote this poem. I was on a flight from Milan, Italy to Dusseldorf, Germany, and as were passing over the vast mountain ranges that comprise the Alps, I couldn't help but think about his wartime experiences. The poem was my sincere yet feeble attempt to connect with what he had endured. I knew I could never fully grasp during a single peacetime flight the anxiety and fear he must have felt when he and his crewmates flew this same space during the war, but I wanted to make an attempt. This poem was intended to pay homage to the bravery and sacrifice of the men from a selfless generation of World War II veterans.

These are the skies,
The same skies you came to know so very well.
As we fly over the same mountains,
The same railroads,
Over the same European land about which you have written,
I try to understand.

The small concern I have now for a safe flight,
No different from any flight,
Seems insignificant compared to what you must have felt during
each mission.
It bothers me that I even begin to compare my current traveling
concerns with the danger of your missions
But I try to understand.

I try to push my concern as far as I can take it,
Make it grow into fear,
Have the same thoughts of loved ones far away,
Their futures,
Their presents.
Maybe in that way I can feel what you felt.
Maybe in that way I can come to understand.

I want to fear the same fears,
Hope the same hopes.
I want to hold on to life and living as much as you must have.
I want to reach the same acceptance of my mortality
And the peace this brings.
I want to be back with the ones I love.

On the ground, I will walk through rebuilt cities,
Become friends with a German man.
"The streets of Dusseldorf are wider than they were before the
war," he says.

"These Are the Skies"

The new Dusseldorf handles the traffic well,
But it lacks the old world charm you expect to find in any Euro-
pean city or town.
My friend accepts the new Dusseldorf.
Its death gave it new life.

The best we can hope to gain from war is not victory,
But peace,
Healing from the pain,
Rebuilding from the destruction,
Life from death.

This will be as close to war as I will ever come,
Flying over an area of conflict some 45 years earlier.
It helps me understand.

Larry Dykstra (1990)

larry.v.dykstra@gmail.com

www.ingramcontent.com/pod-product-compliance
Lightning Source LLC
Chambersburg PA
CBHW070122100426
42744CB00010B/1903